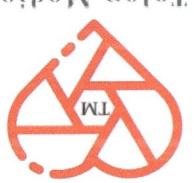

Tolen Media

A COLLECTION OF FAMOUS QUOTES
AND ORIGINAL PHOTOGRAPHY FROM
CHRISTOPHER CONRAD TOLEN

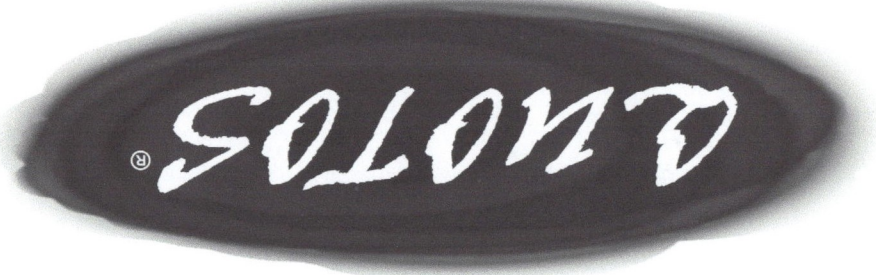

Copyright © 2020 by Tolen Media

All rights reserved.

This book or any portion thereof
may not be reproduced or used in any manner whatsoever
without the express written permission of the publisher
except for the use of brief quotations in a book review.

Printed in the United States of America
ISBN: 978-1-65825-414-4
First Printing, 2020

@tolenmedia
www.tolen.media
tolenmedia@gmail.com

I dedicate this work to Edward W. Bok, without whose gift to the world, much of this content would not have been possible. Also, to my daughters Ariel and Tessani and my son Elijah. A father couldn't be more proud of who you all are becoming. I hope this collection of some of my travels and art inspires you to move mountains, cross oceans and reach for the stars.

Christopher Conrad Tolen (Jan 7, 2020)

Give to the world the best you have and the best will come back to you.

Edward W Bok

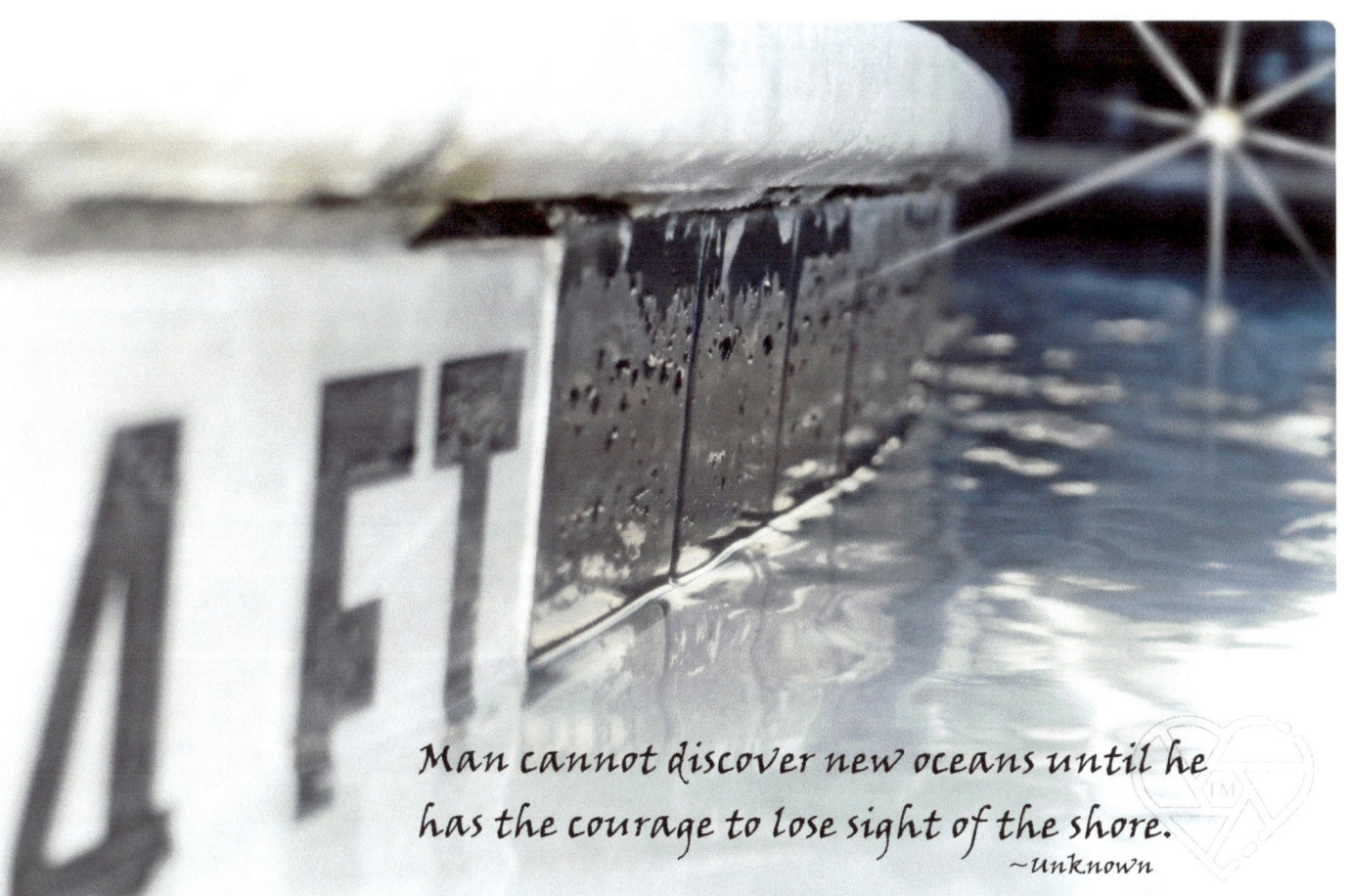

A human being is a single being.

Unique and unrepeatable.

~John Paul II

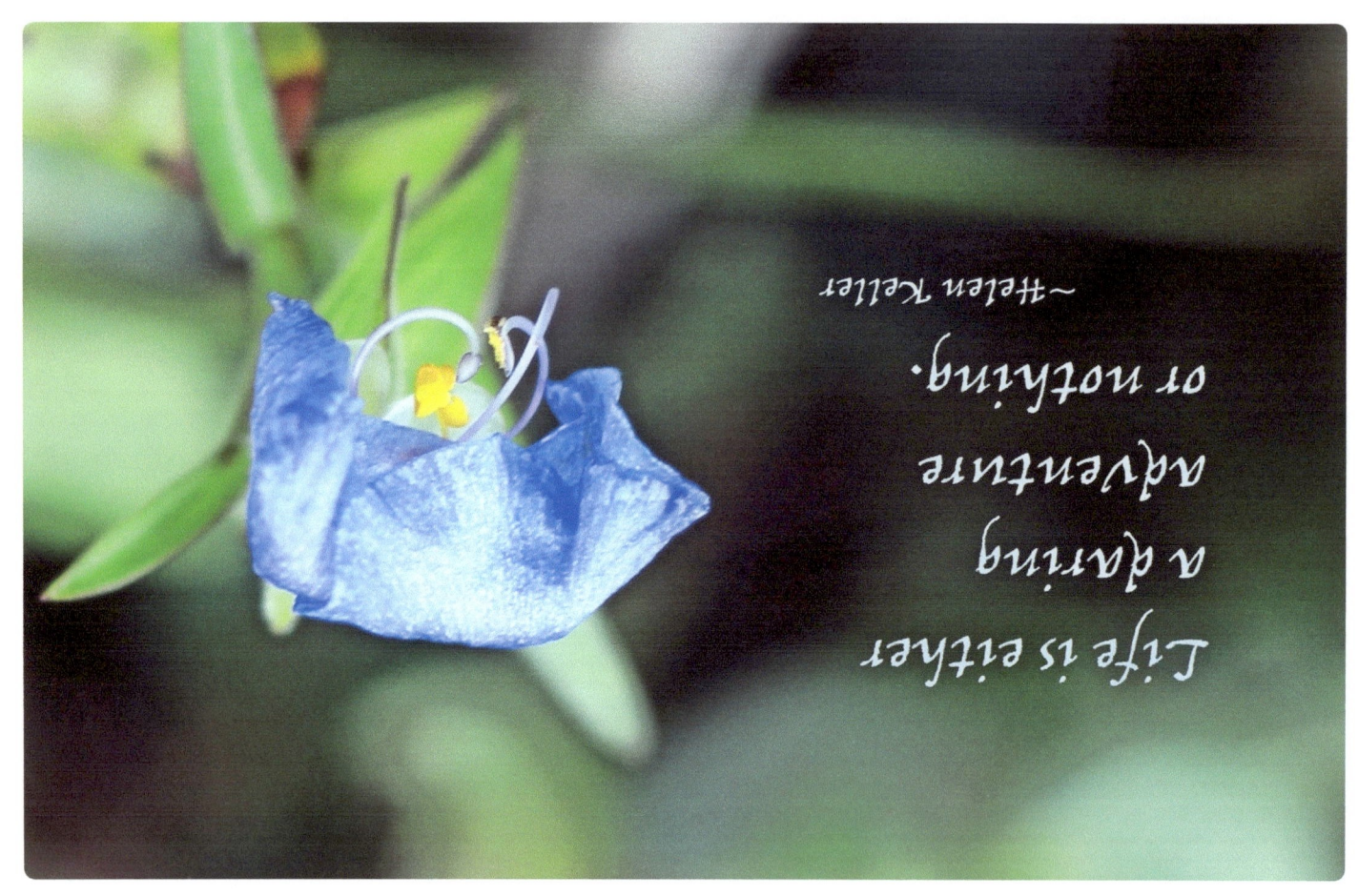

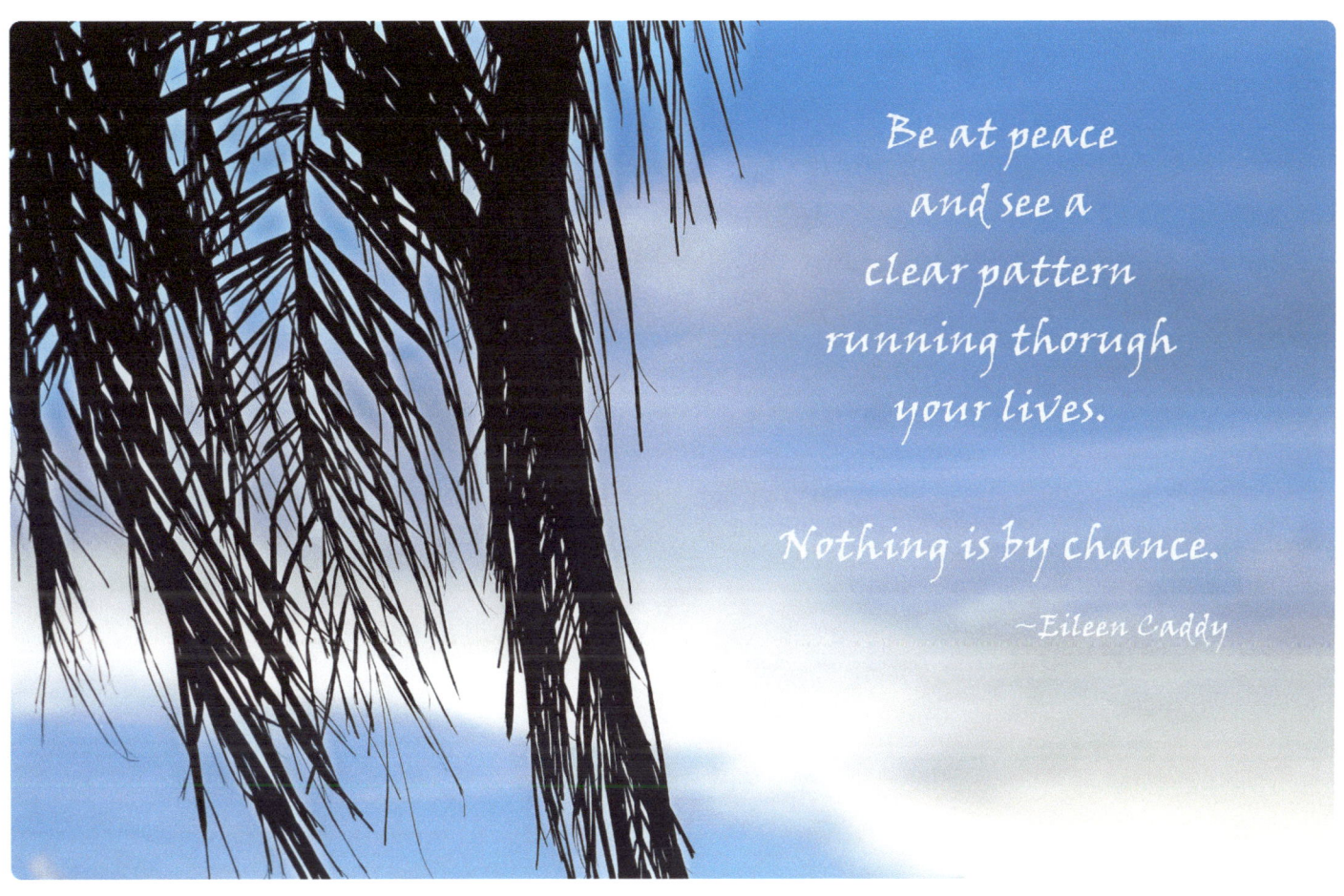

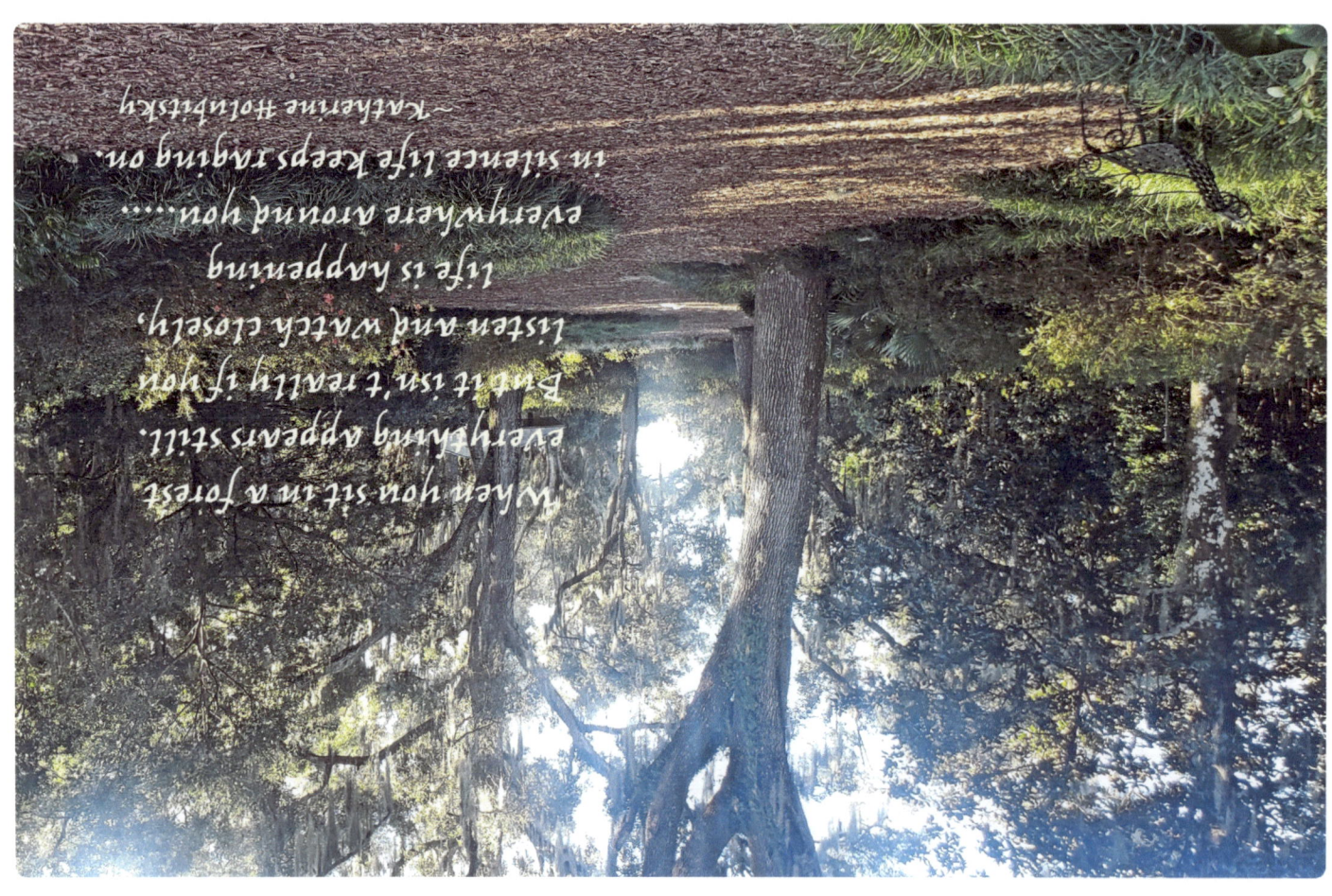

When you sit in a forest
everything appears still.
But it isn't really, if you
listen and watch closely,
life is happening
everywhere around you......
in silence life keeps raging on.
— Katherine Holubitsky

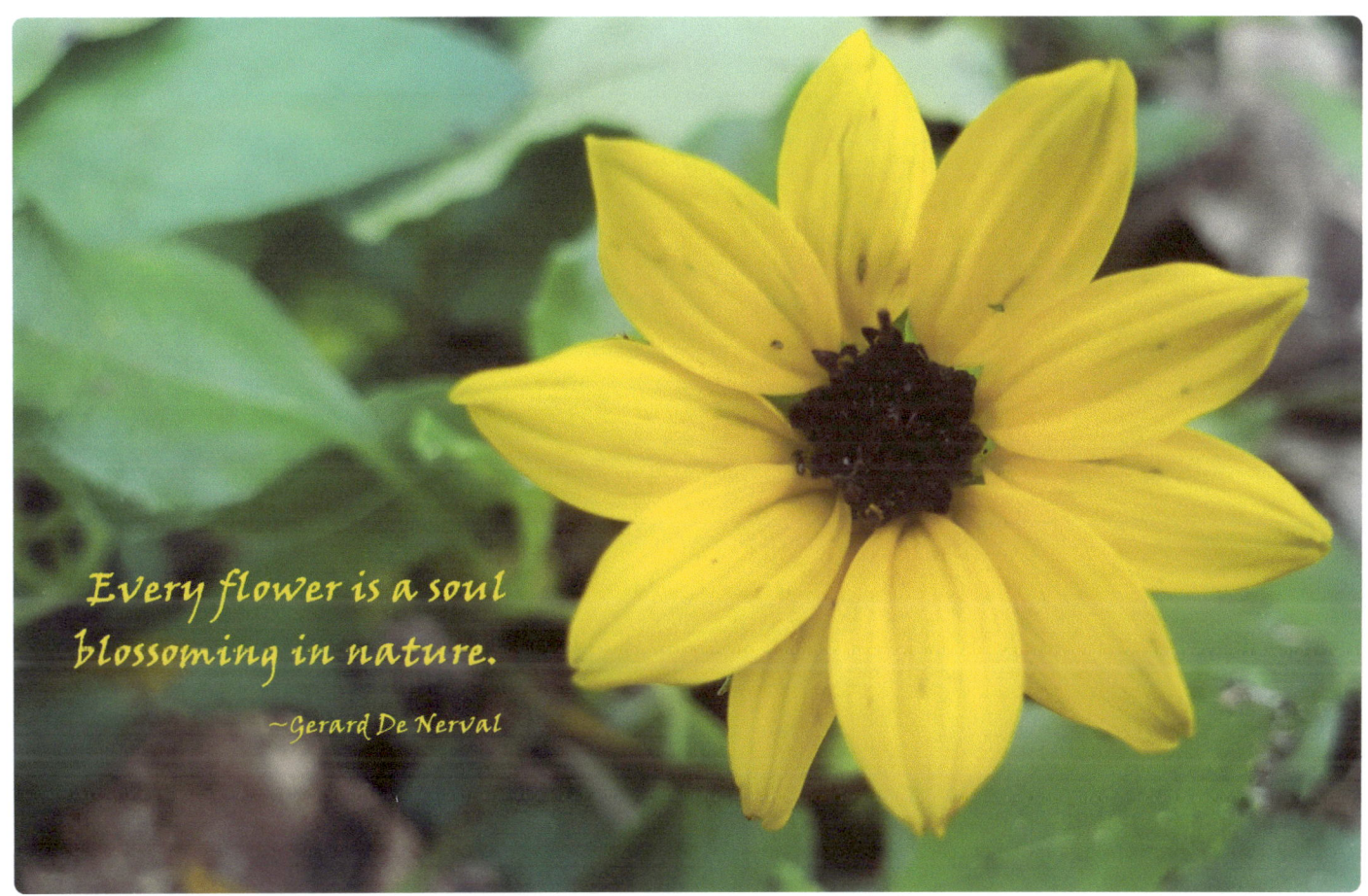

I believe in Liberty for all men: the space to stretch their arms and their souls, the right to breathe and the right to vote, the freedom to choose their friends, enjoy the sunshine, and ride on the railroads, uncursed by color, thinking, dreaming, working as they will in a kingdom of beauty and love.

~W. E. B. Du Bois

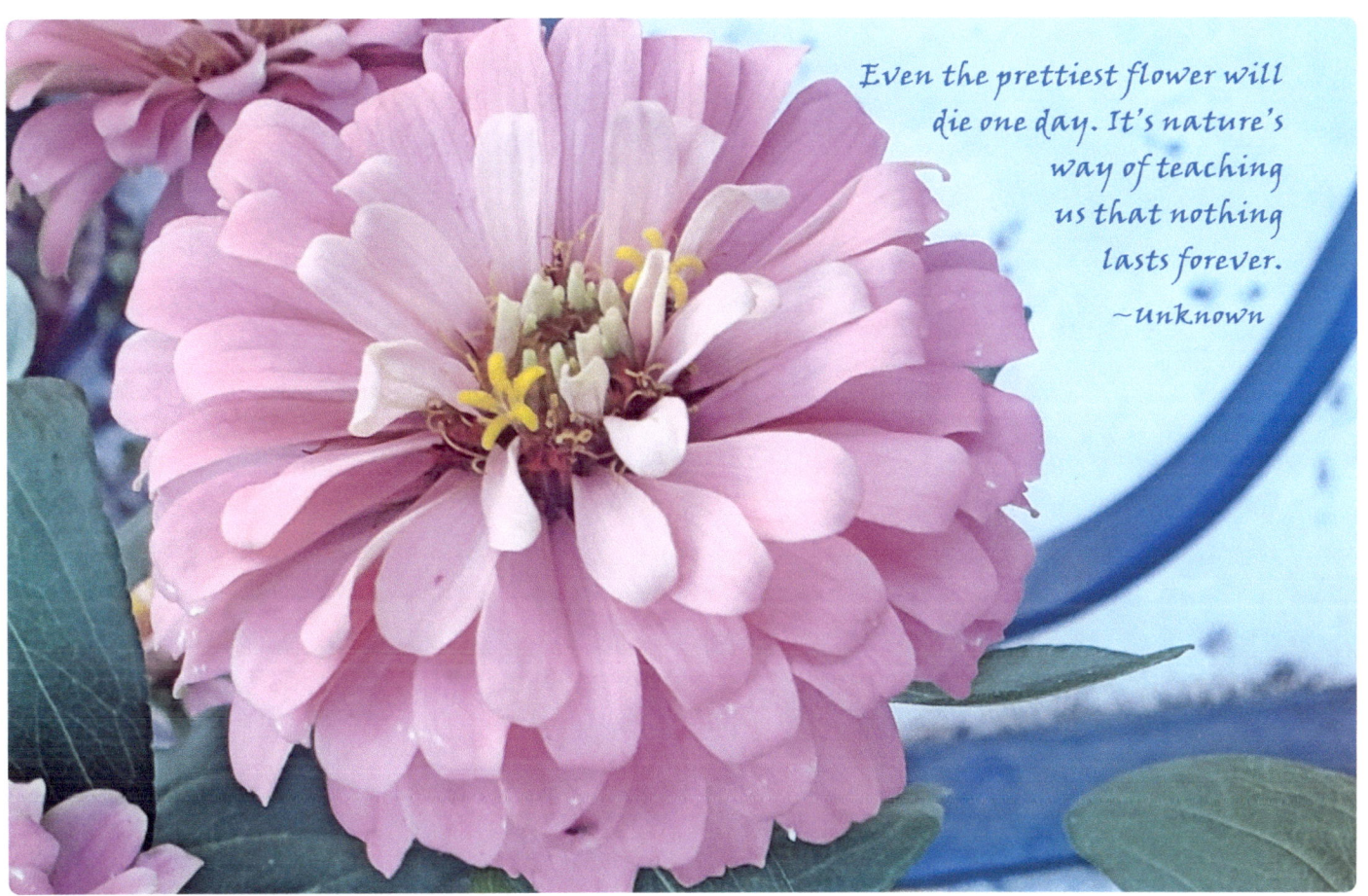

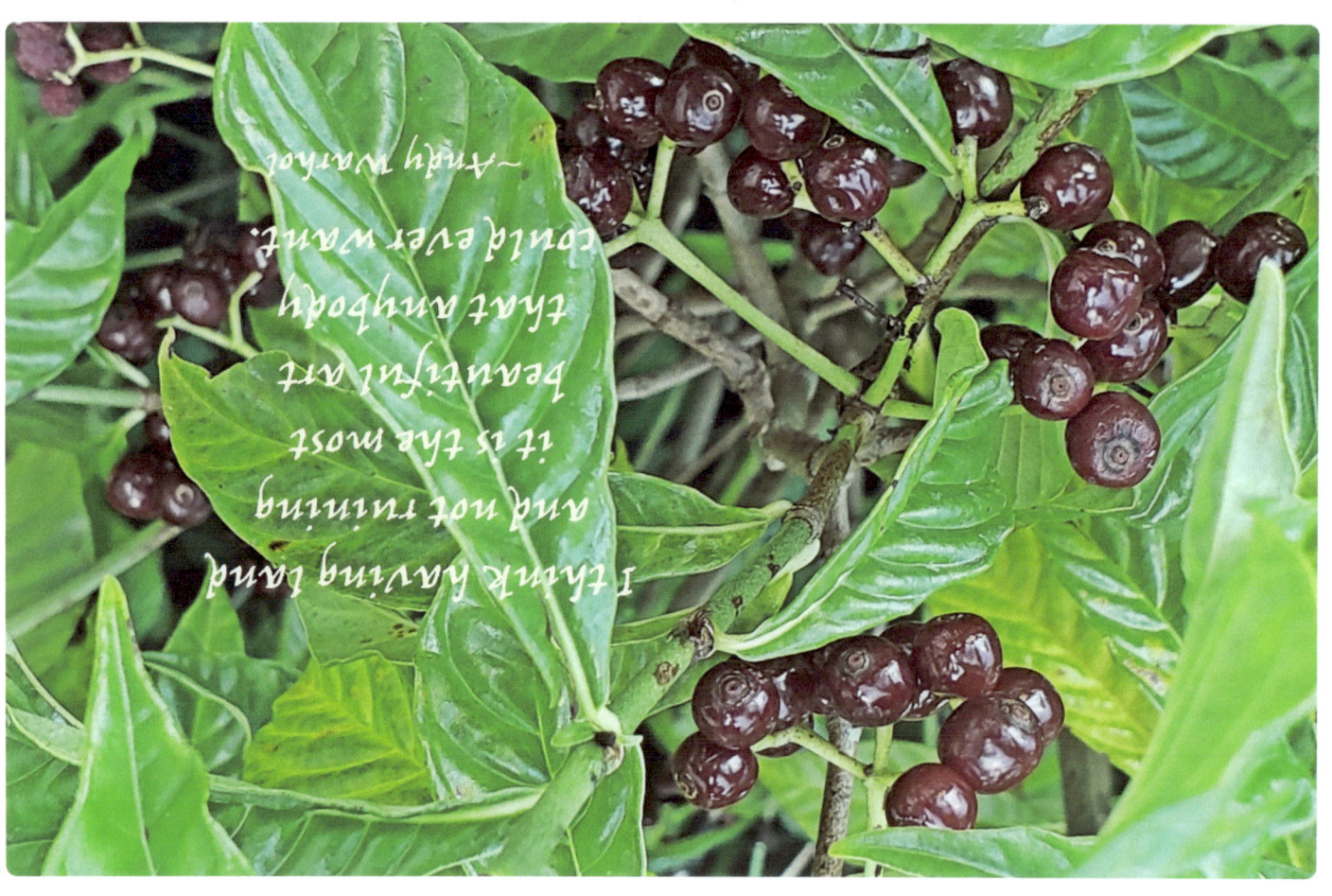

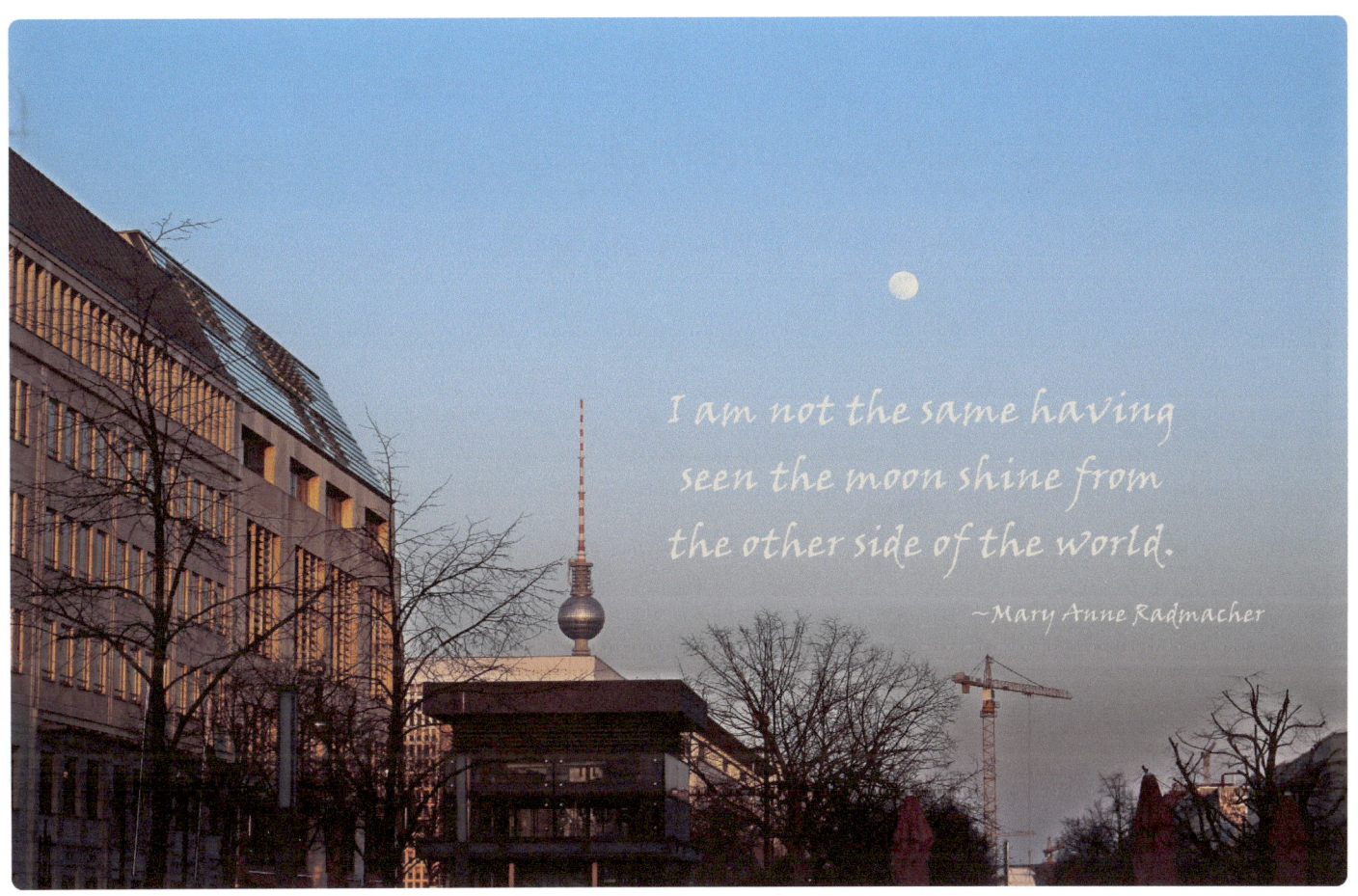

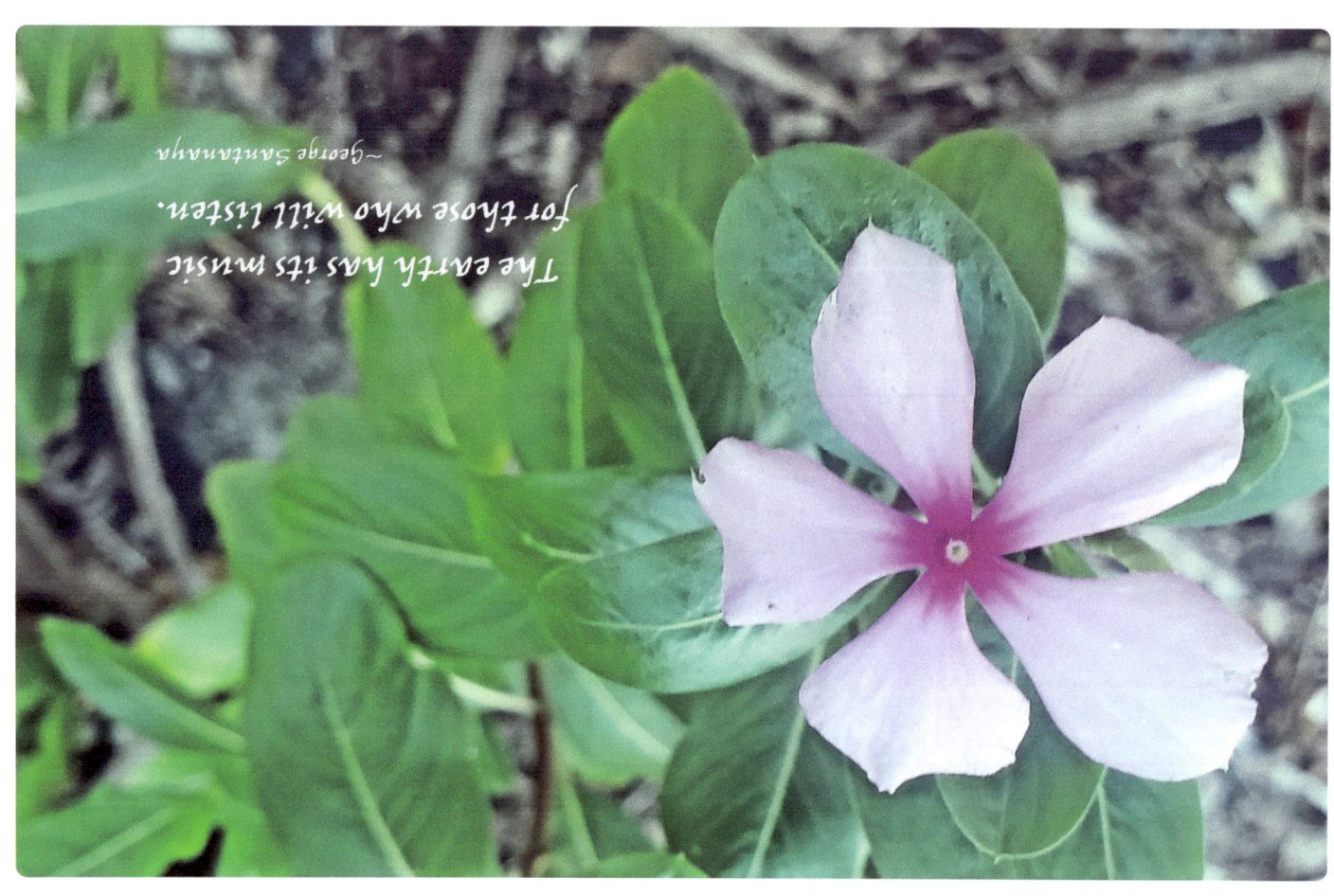

The earth has its music for those who will listen.
~George Santayana

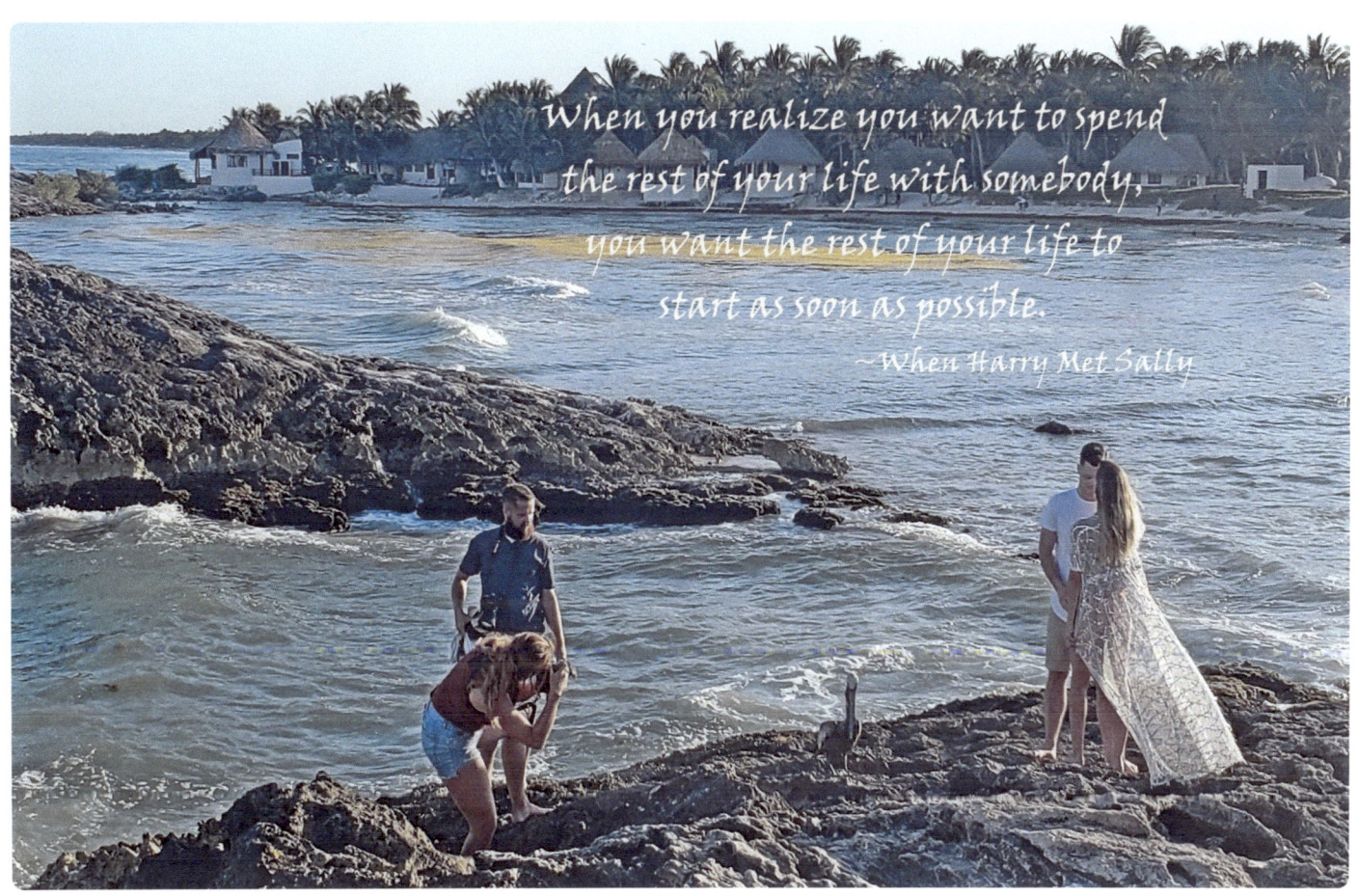

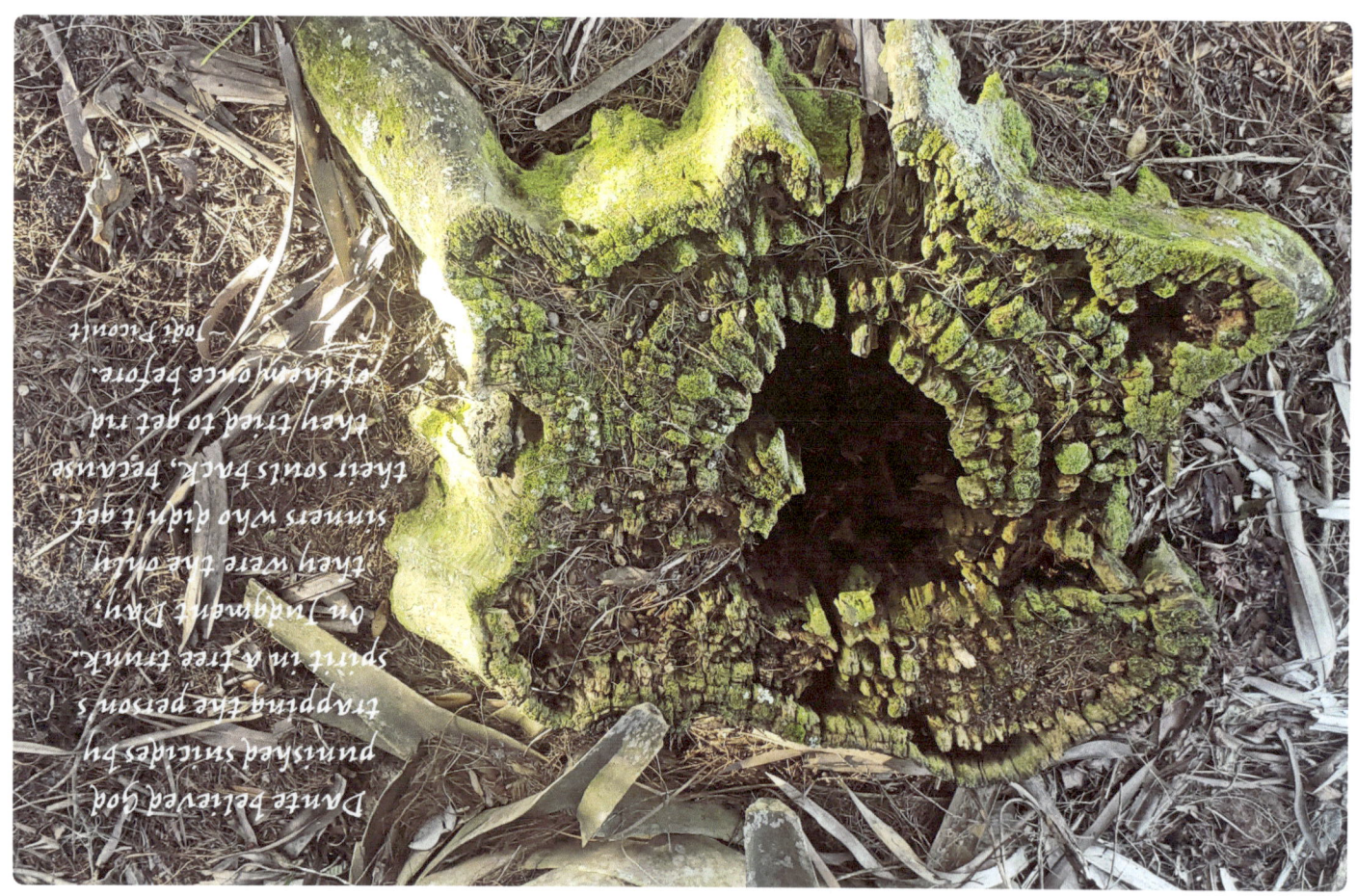

Dante believed God punished suicides by trapping the person's spirit in a tree trunk. On Judgment Day, they were the only sinners who didn't get their souls back, because they tried to get rid of them once before.
—Jodi Picoult

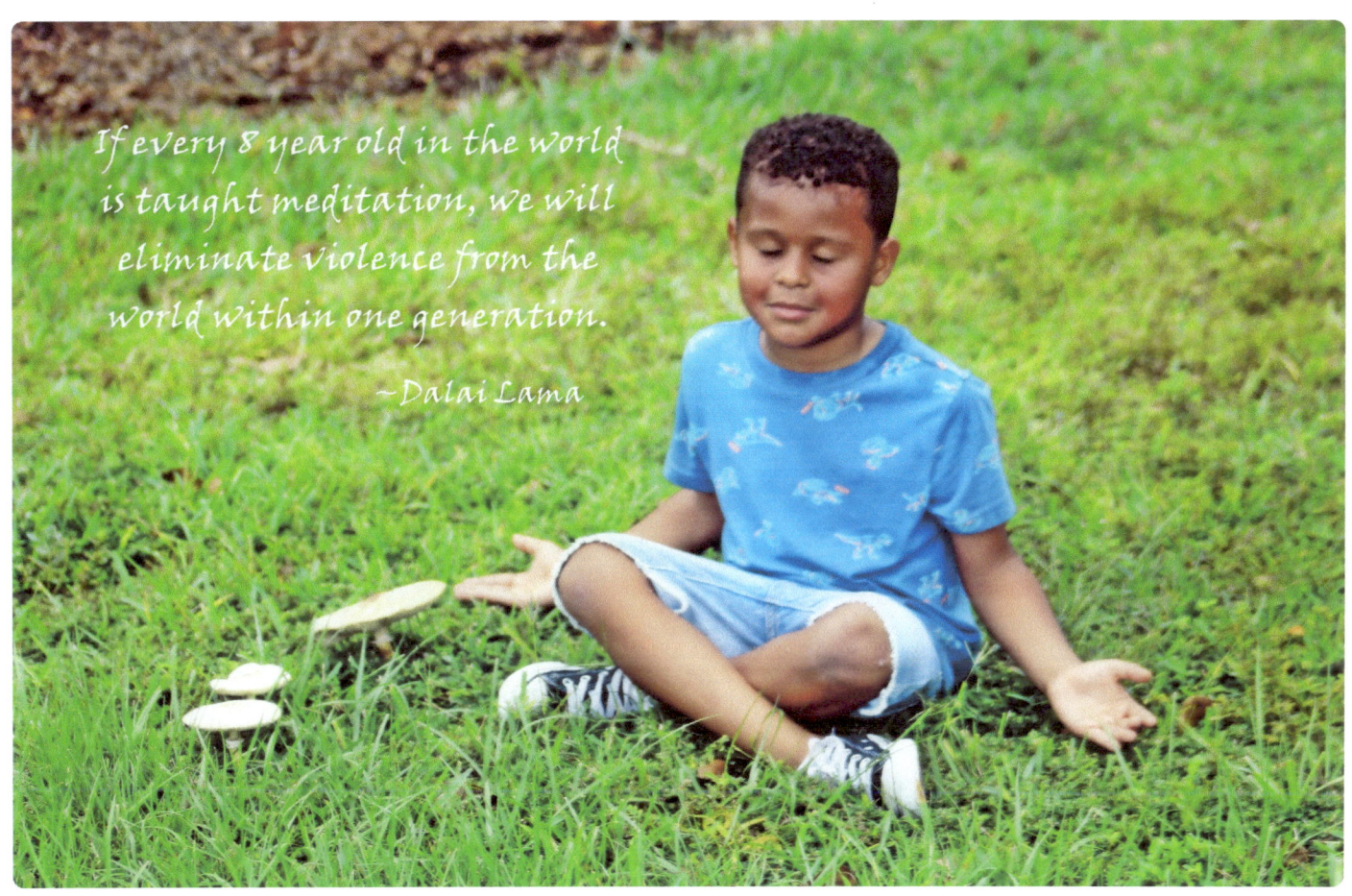

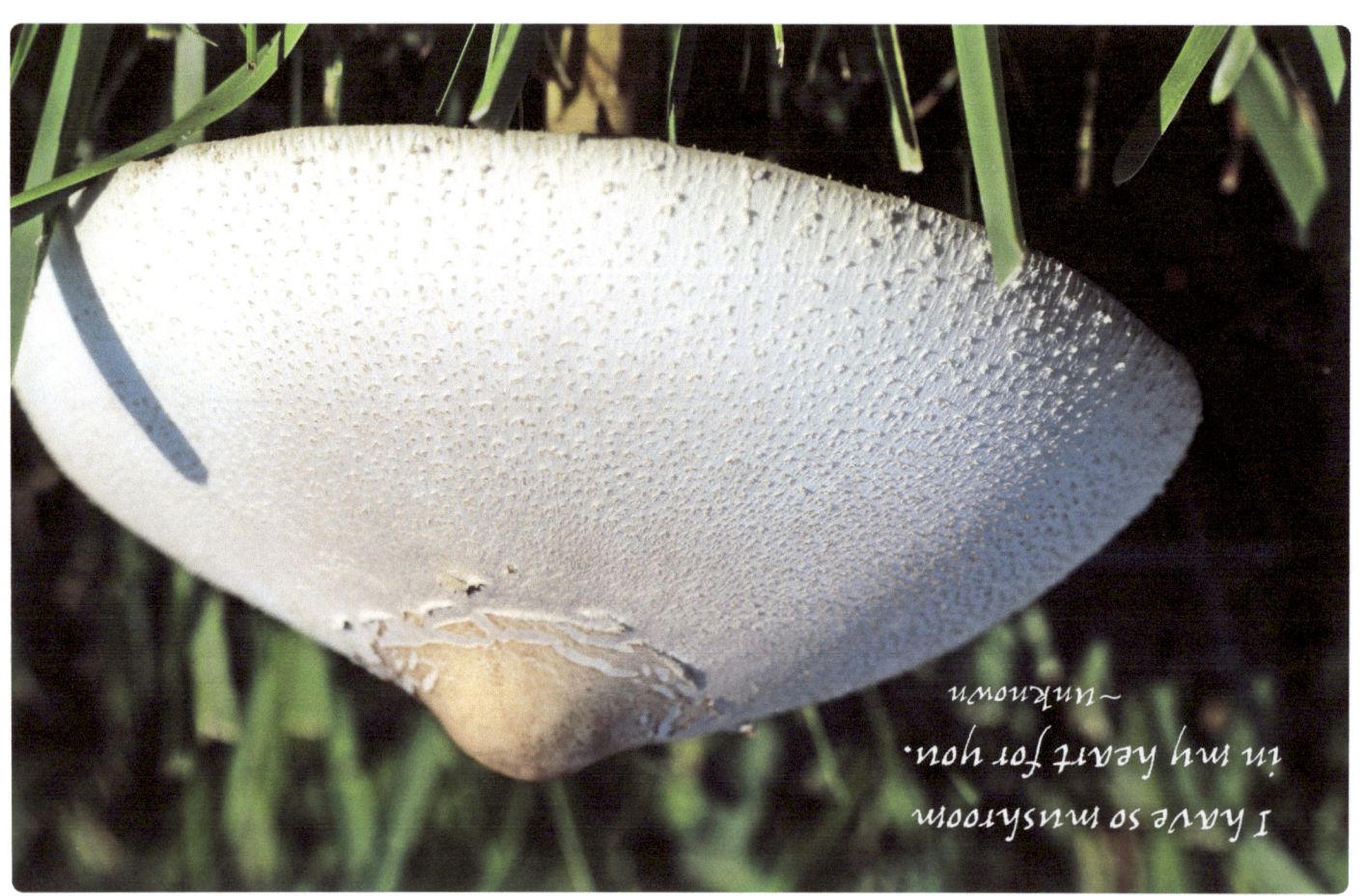

I have so mushroom in my heart for you.
~unknown

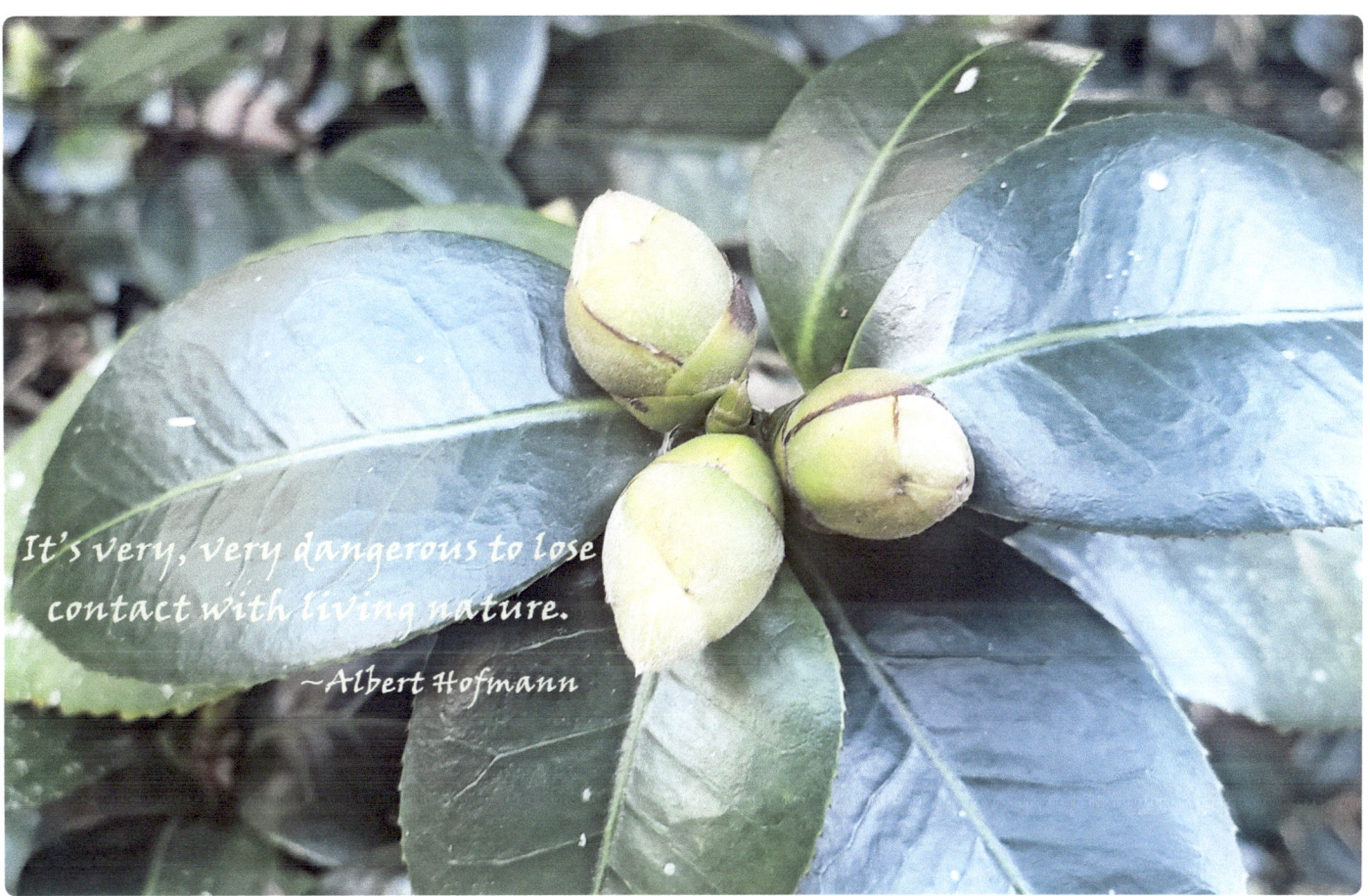

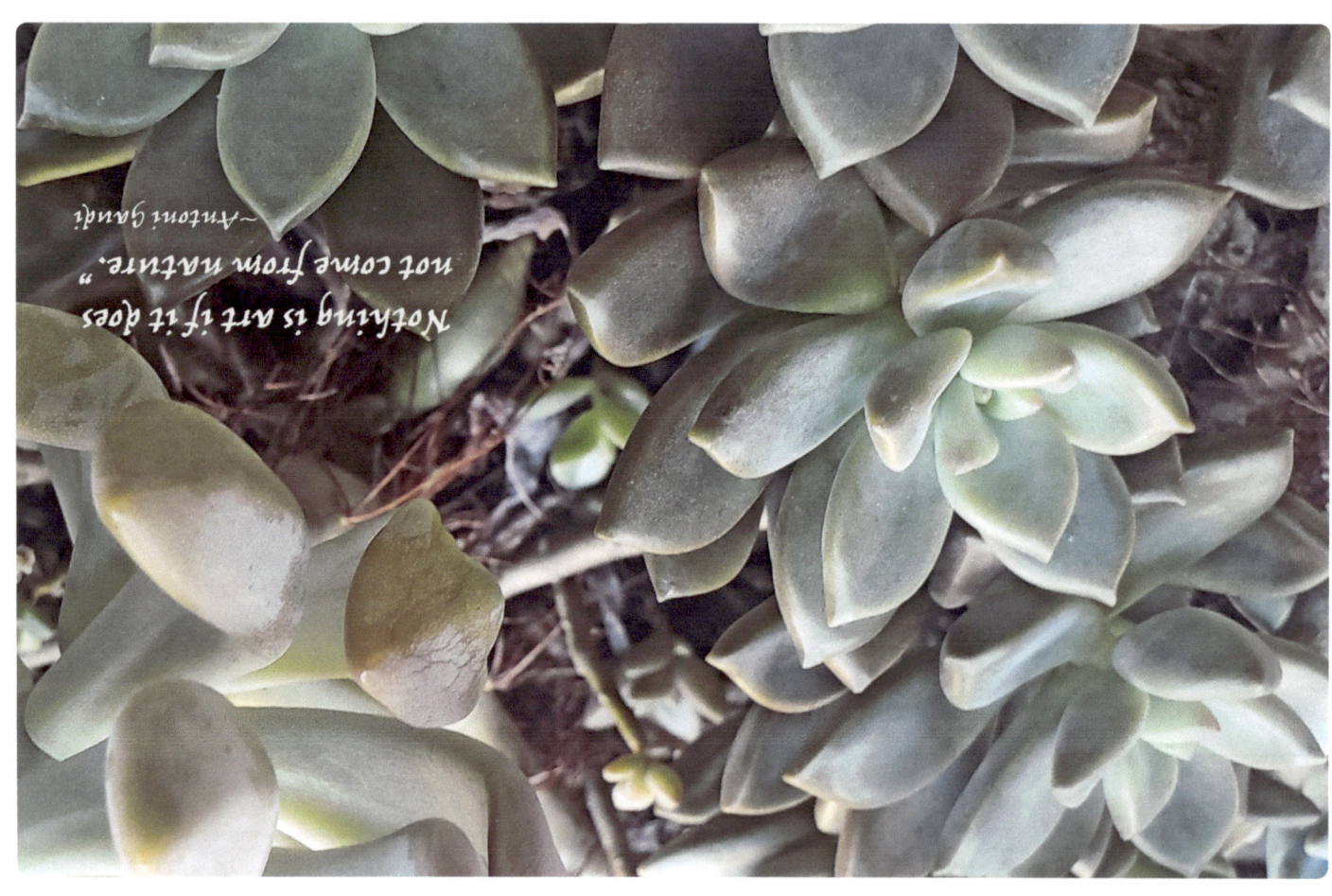

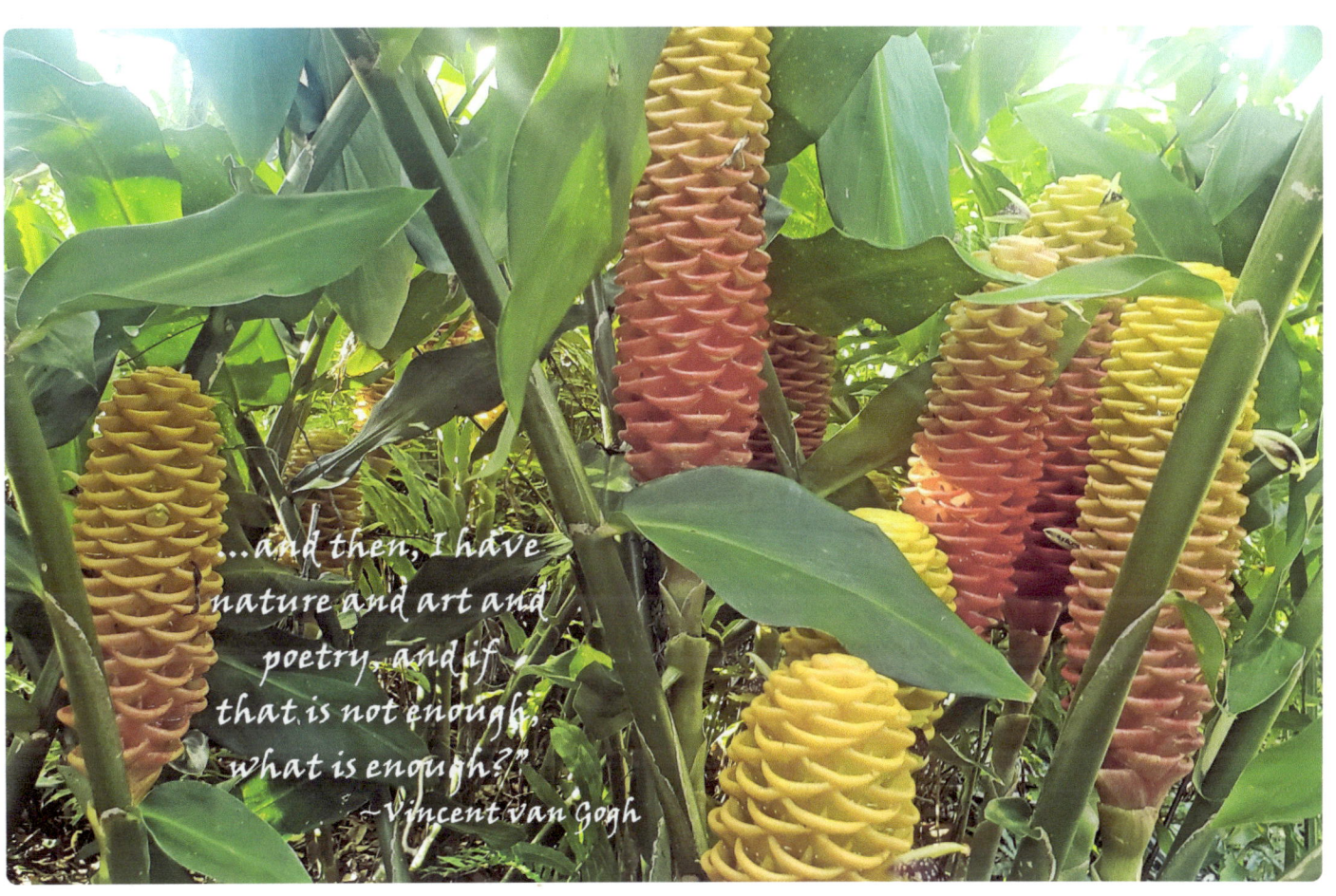

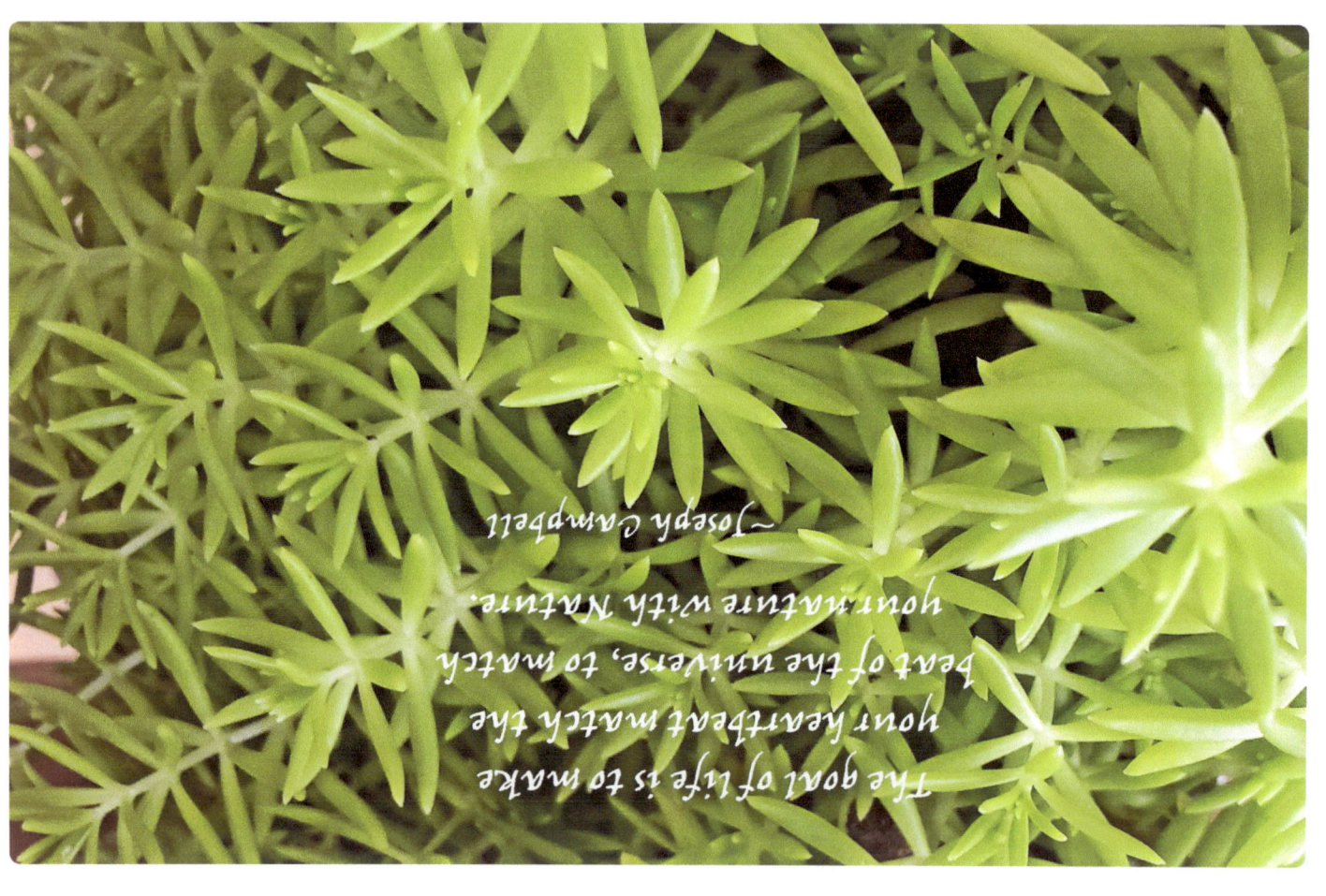

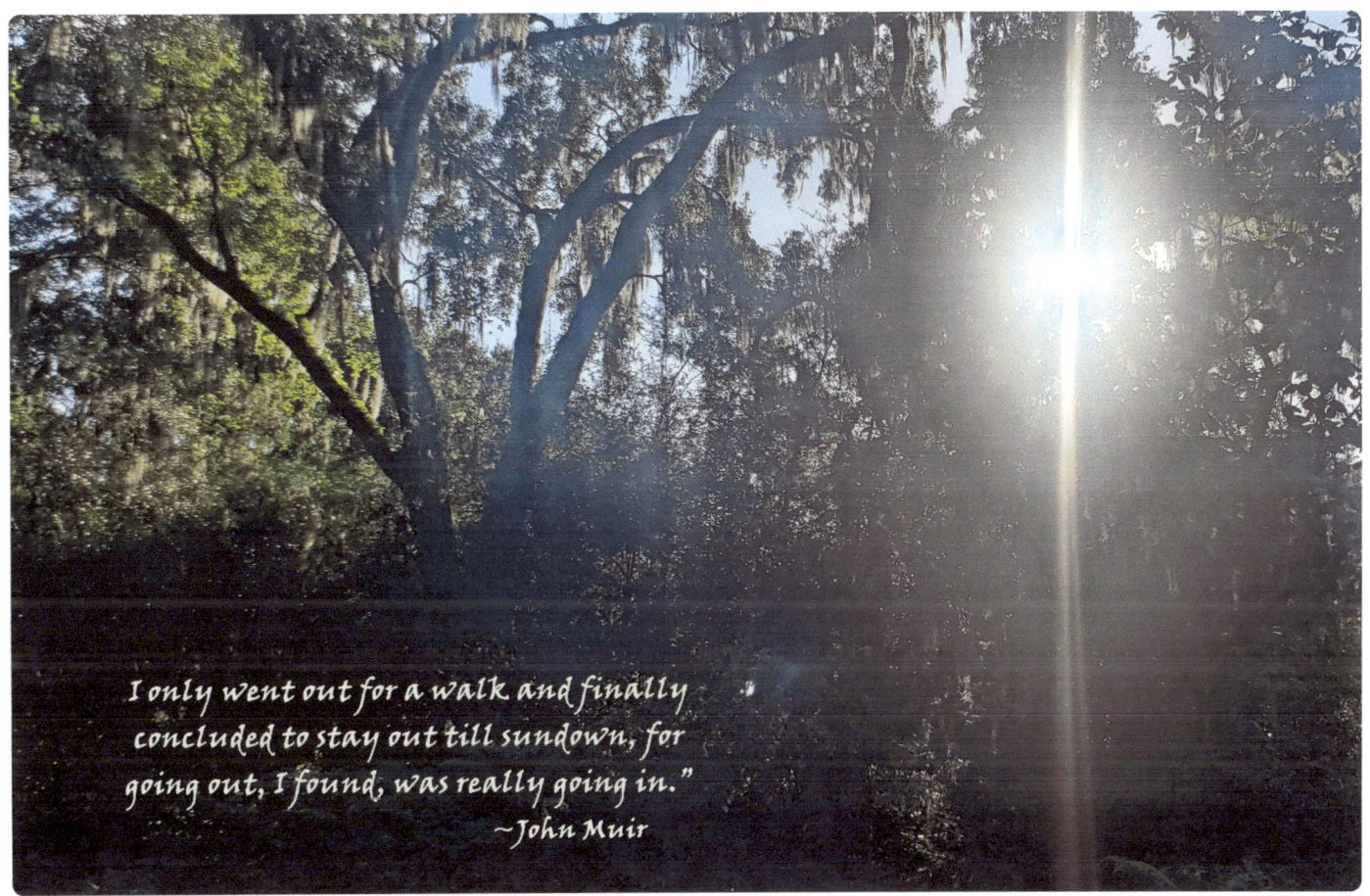

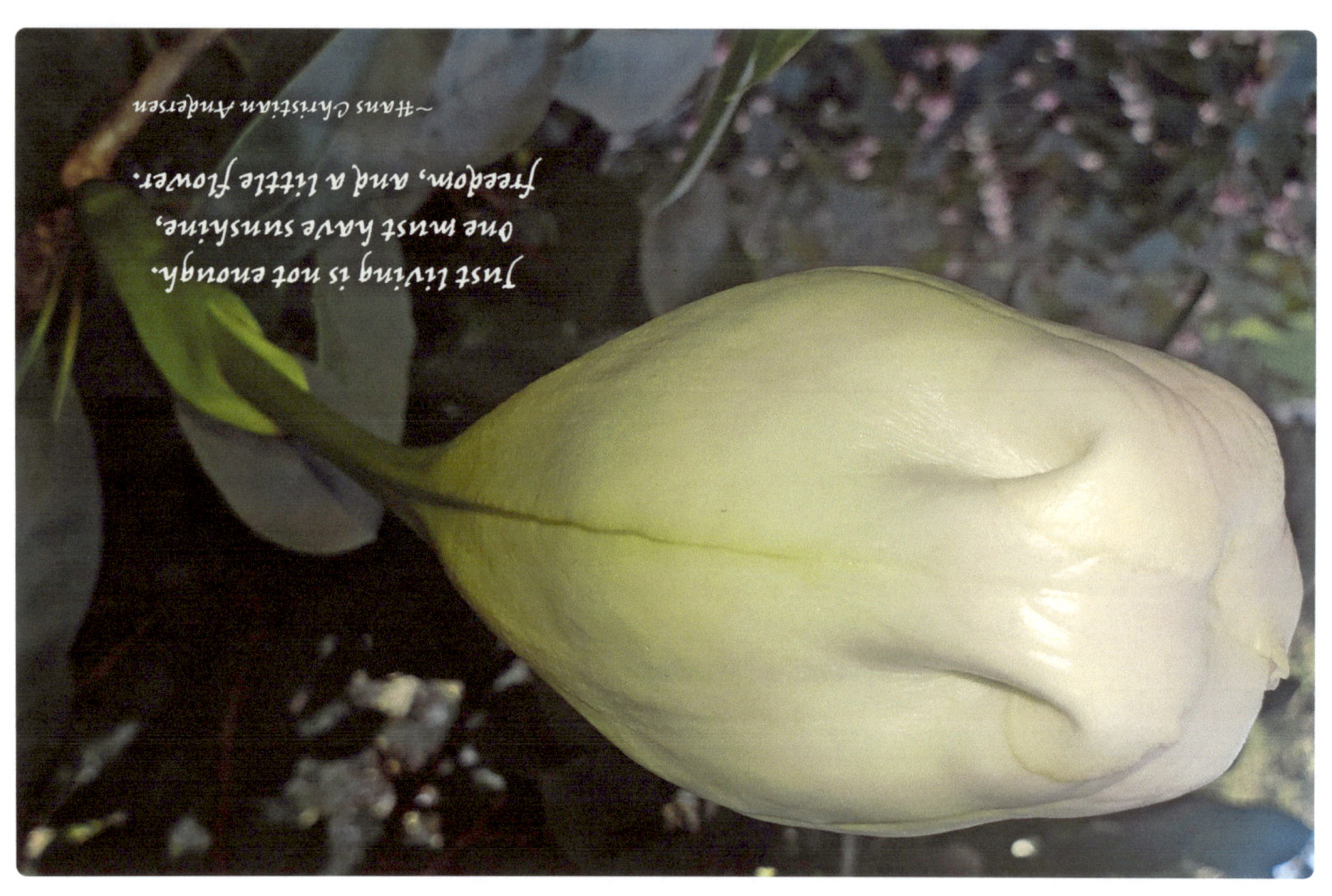

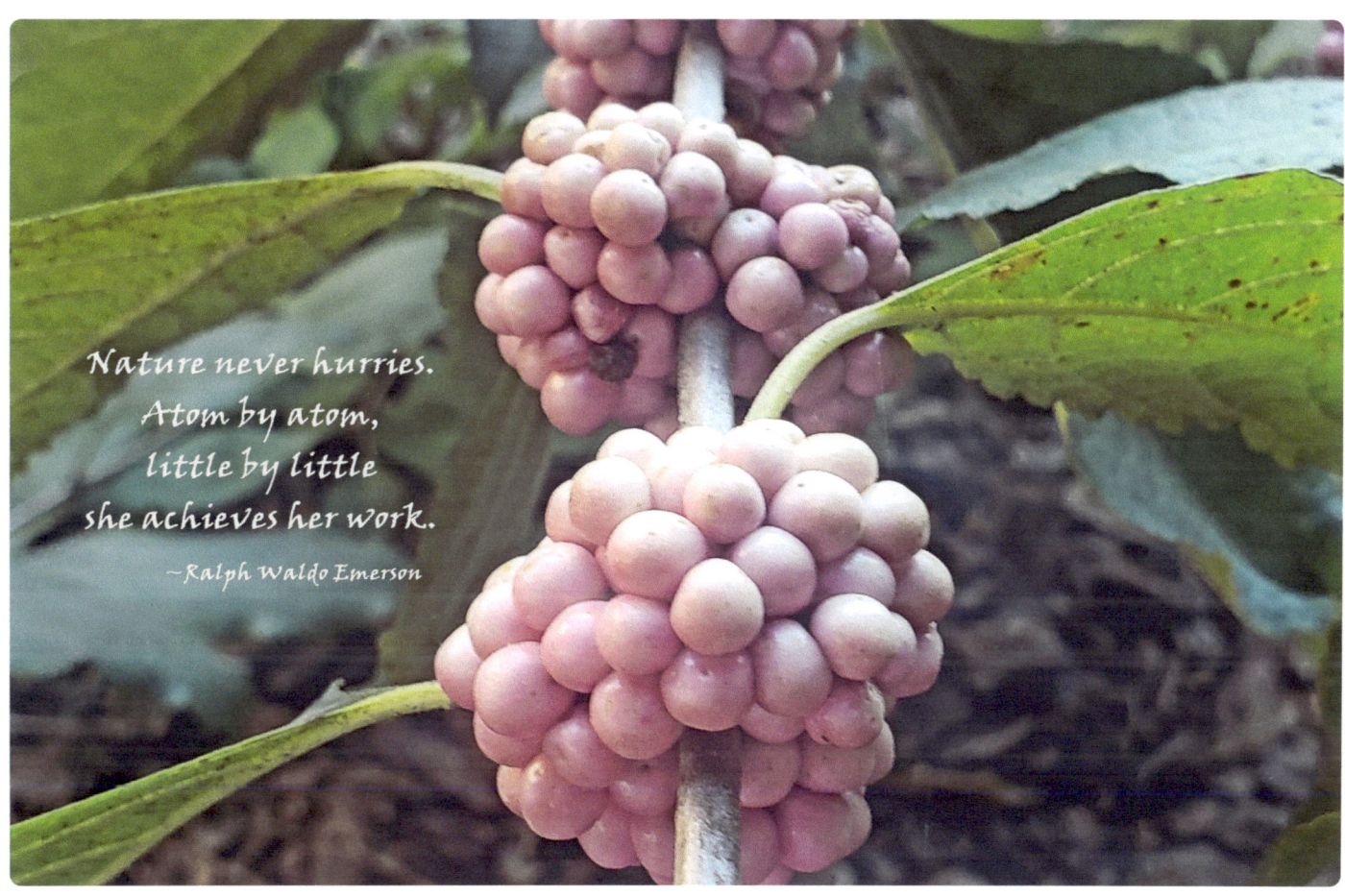

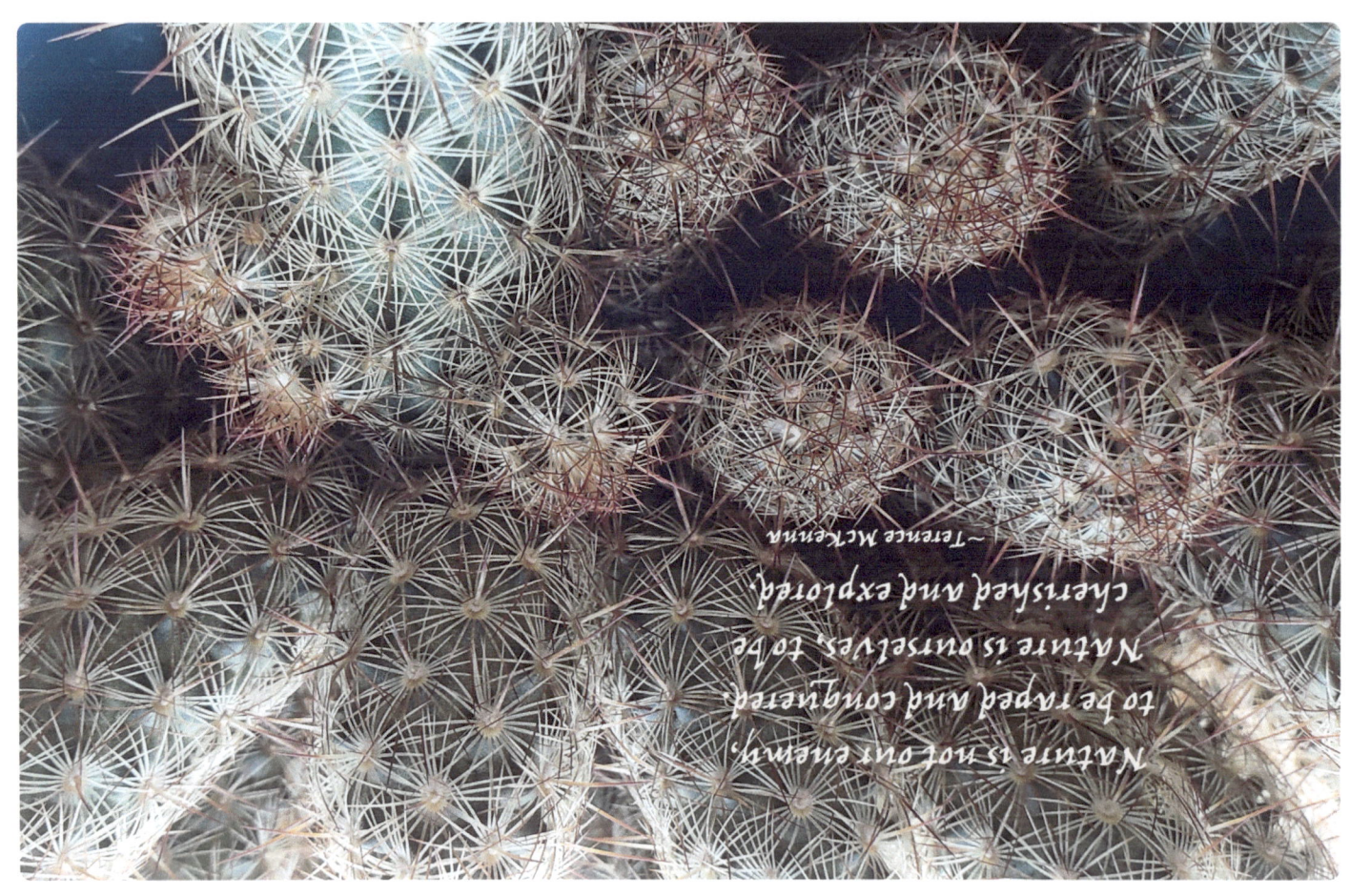

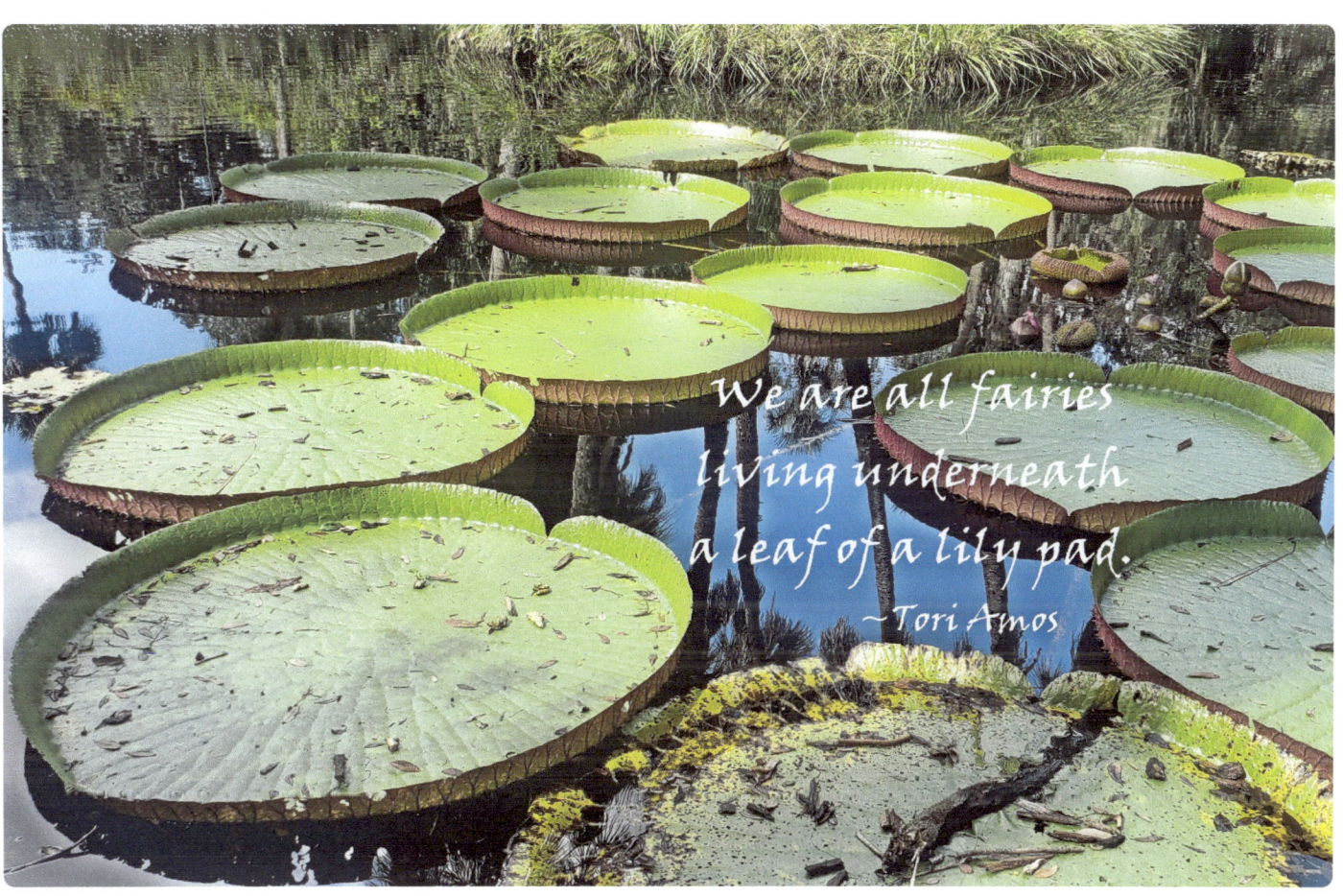

"There is no better designer than nature."
~Alexander McQueen

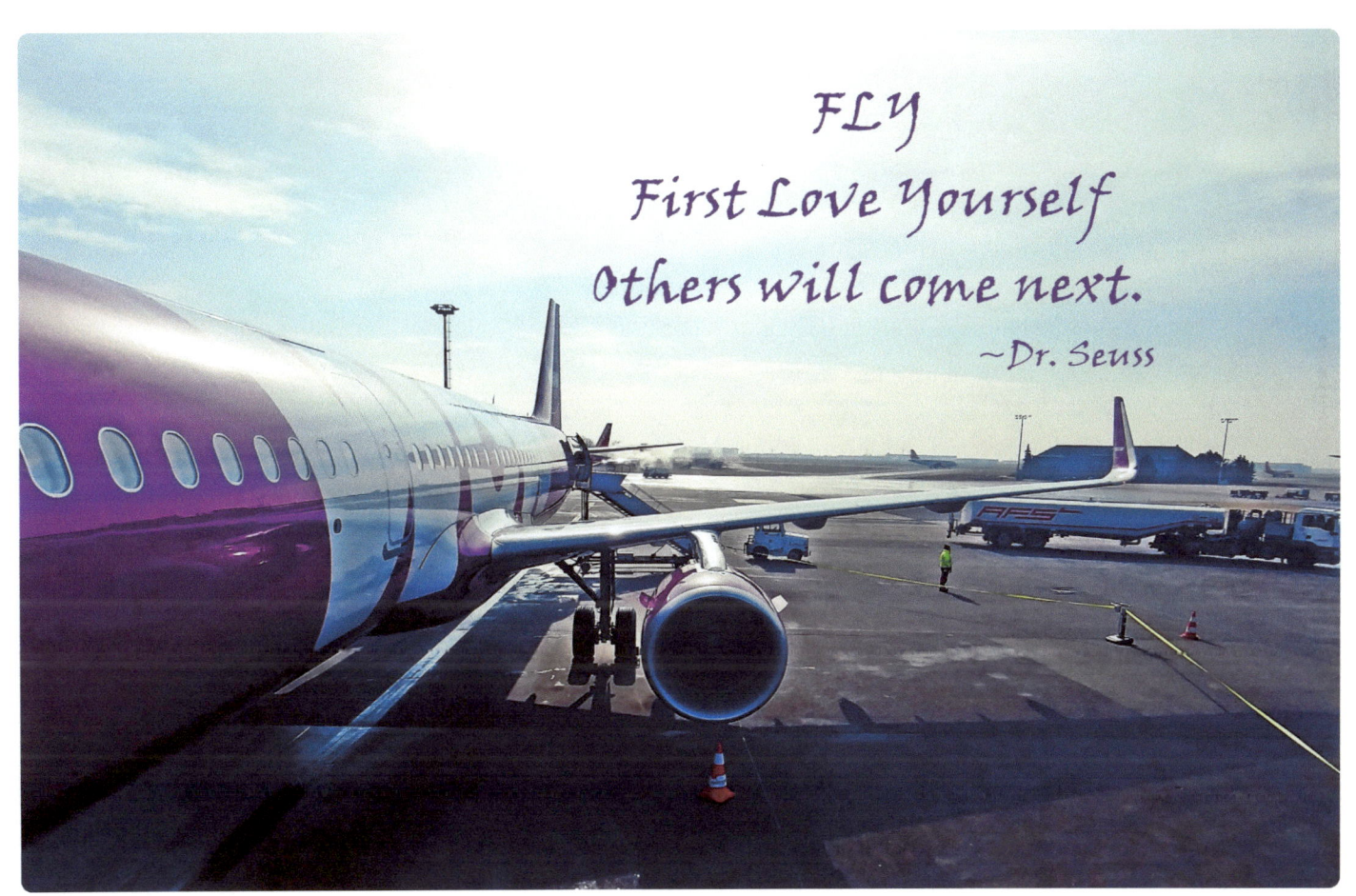

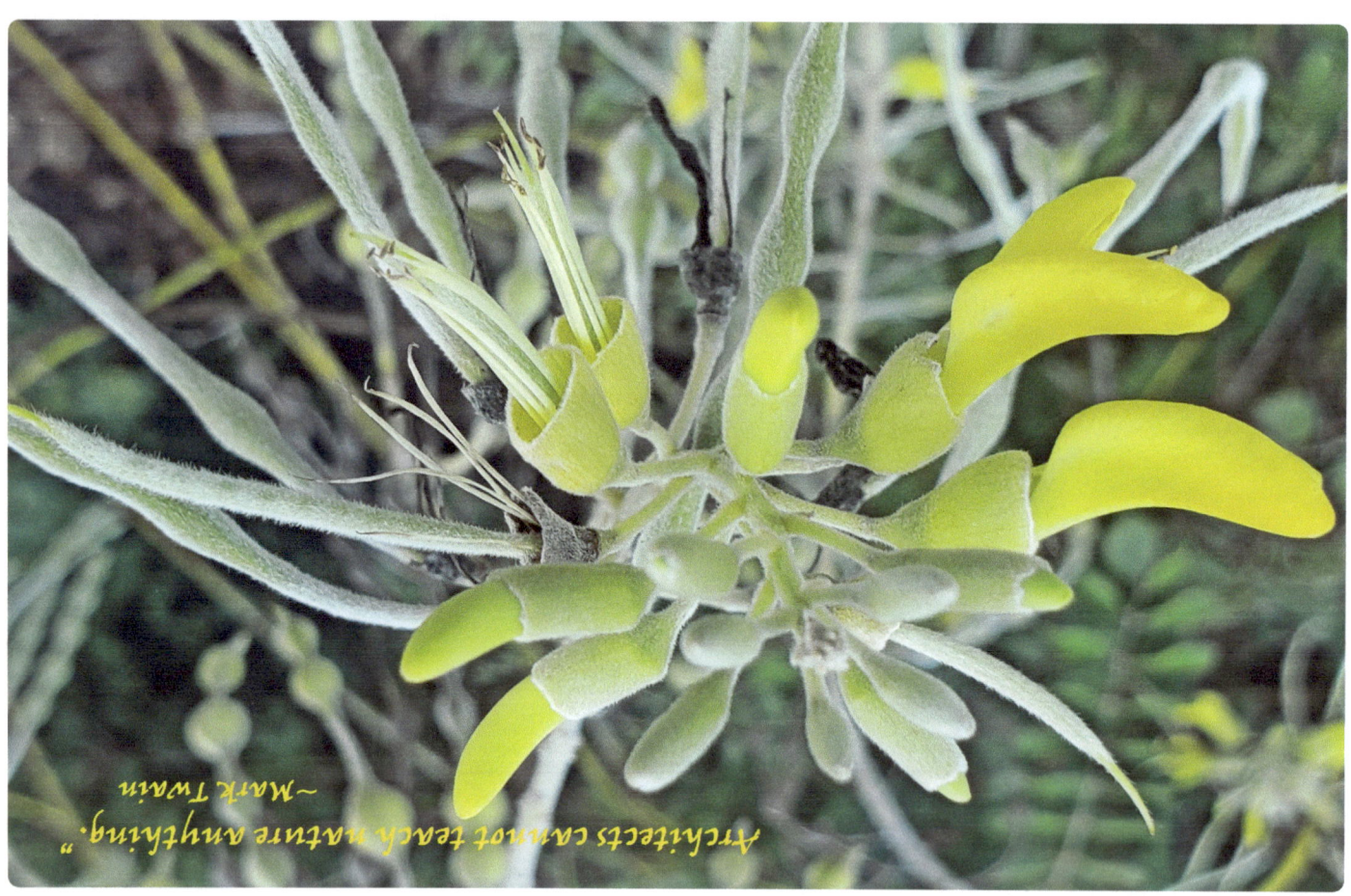

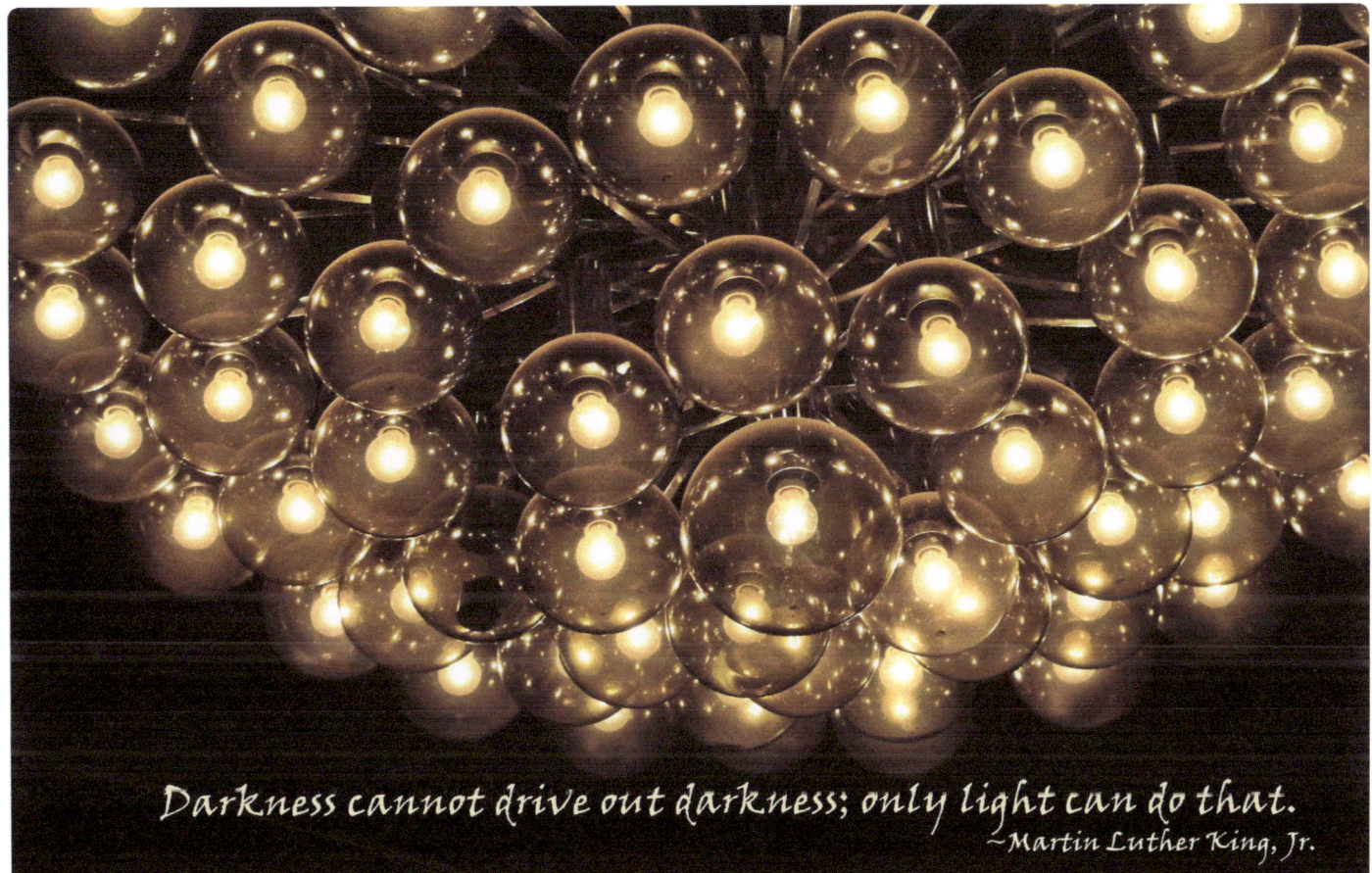

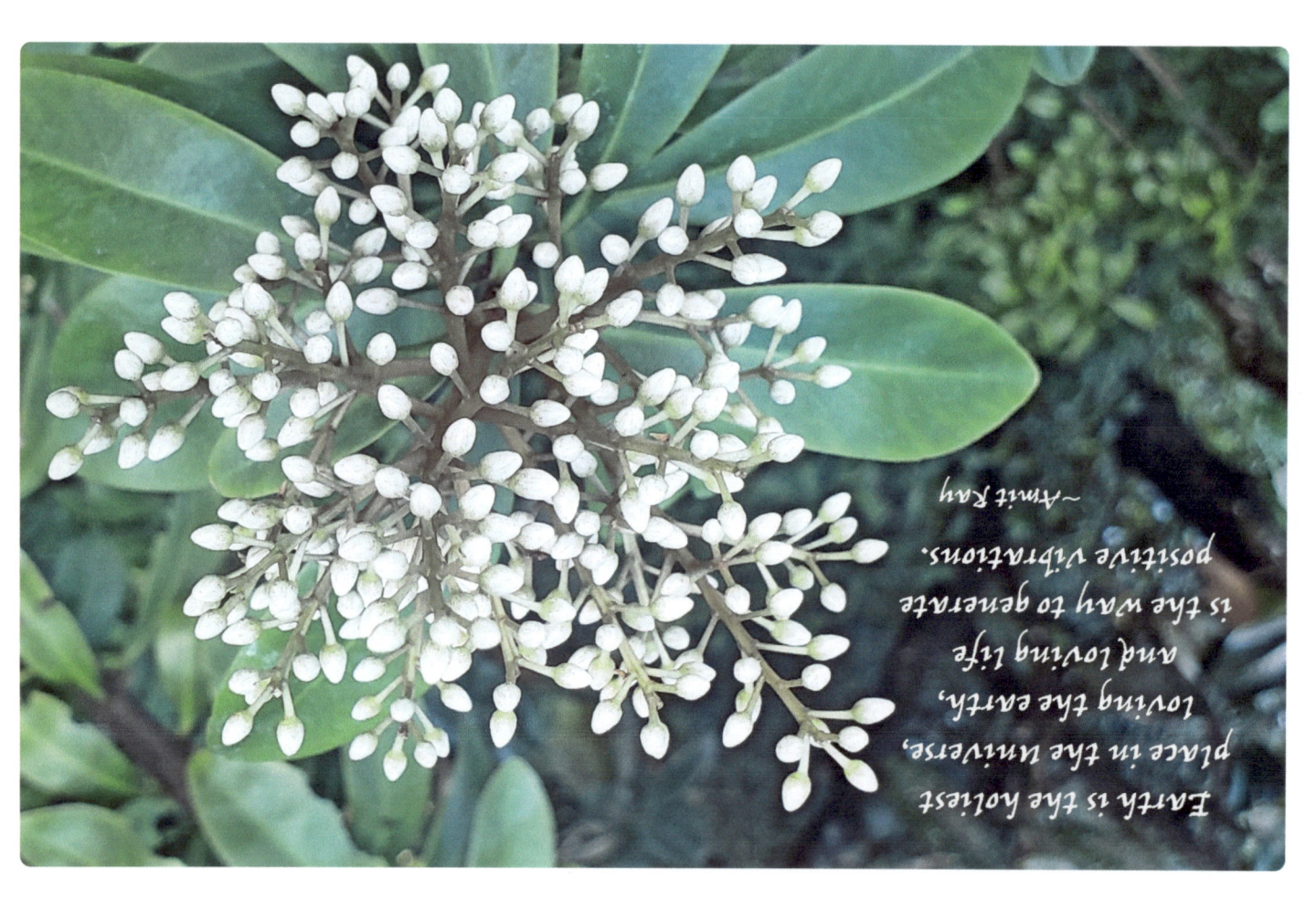

Earth is the holiest place in the universe, loving the earth, and loving life is the way to generate positive vibrations.
~Amit Ray

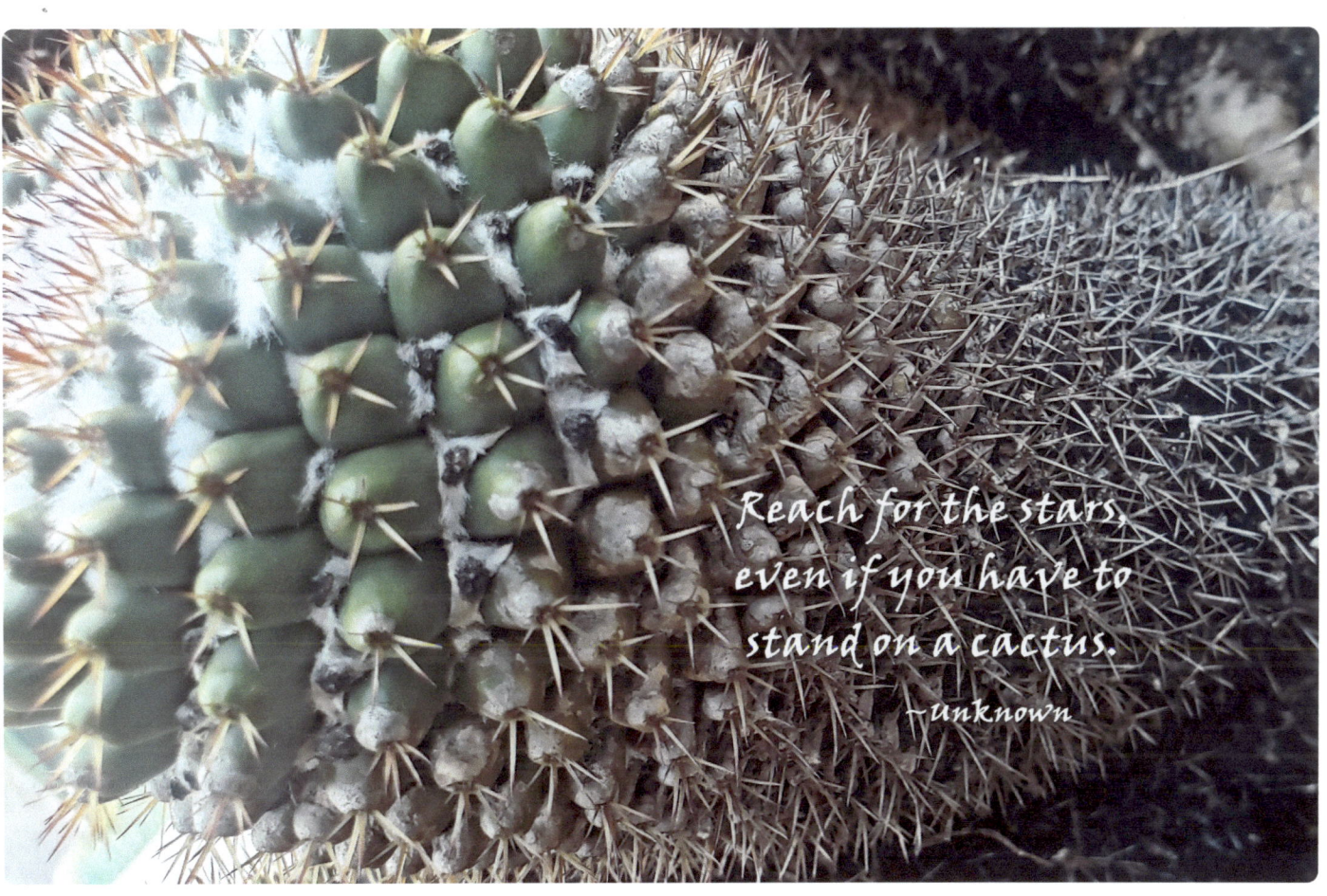

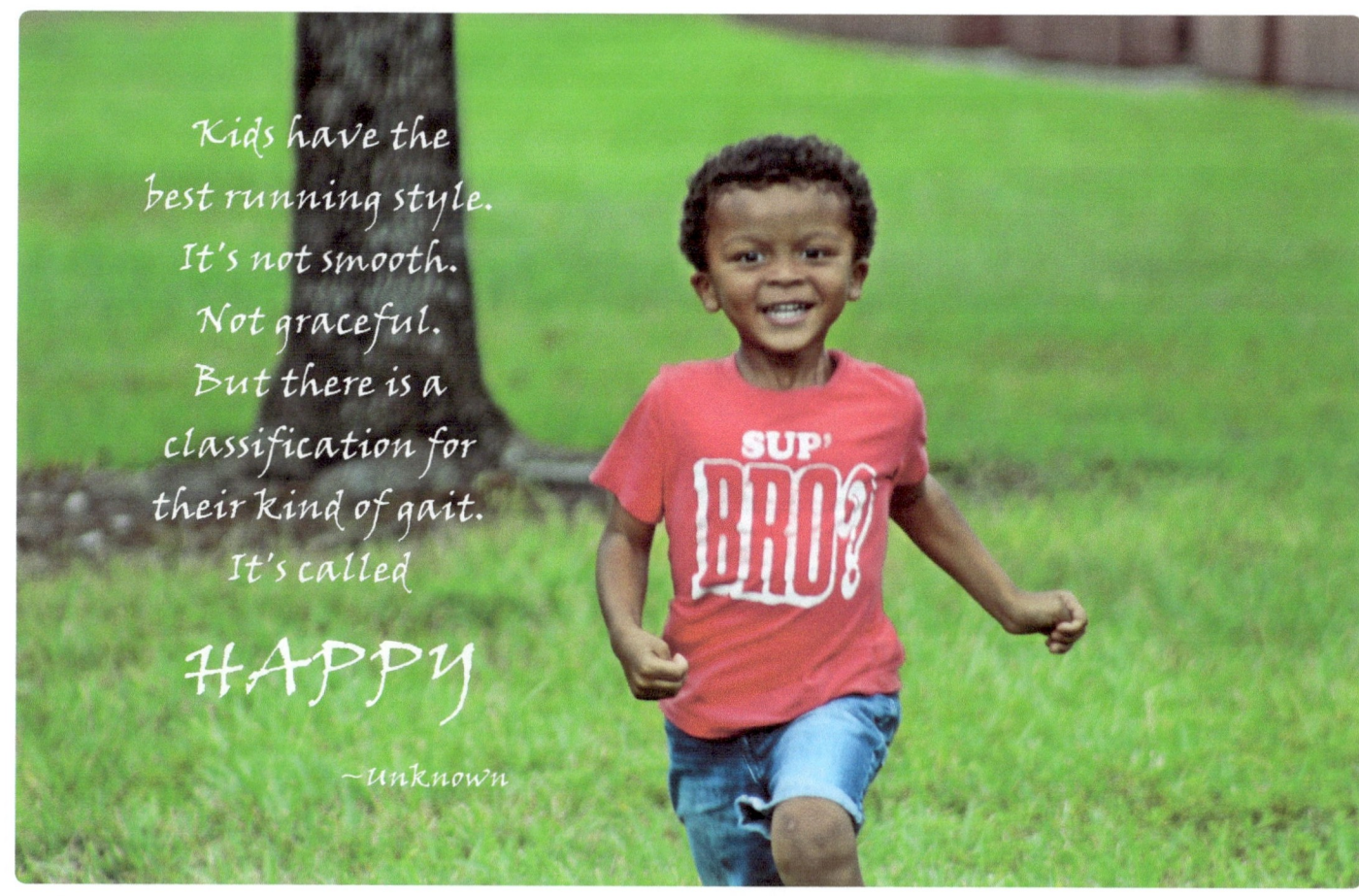

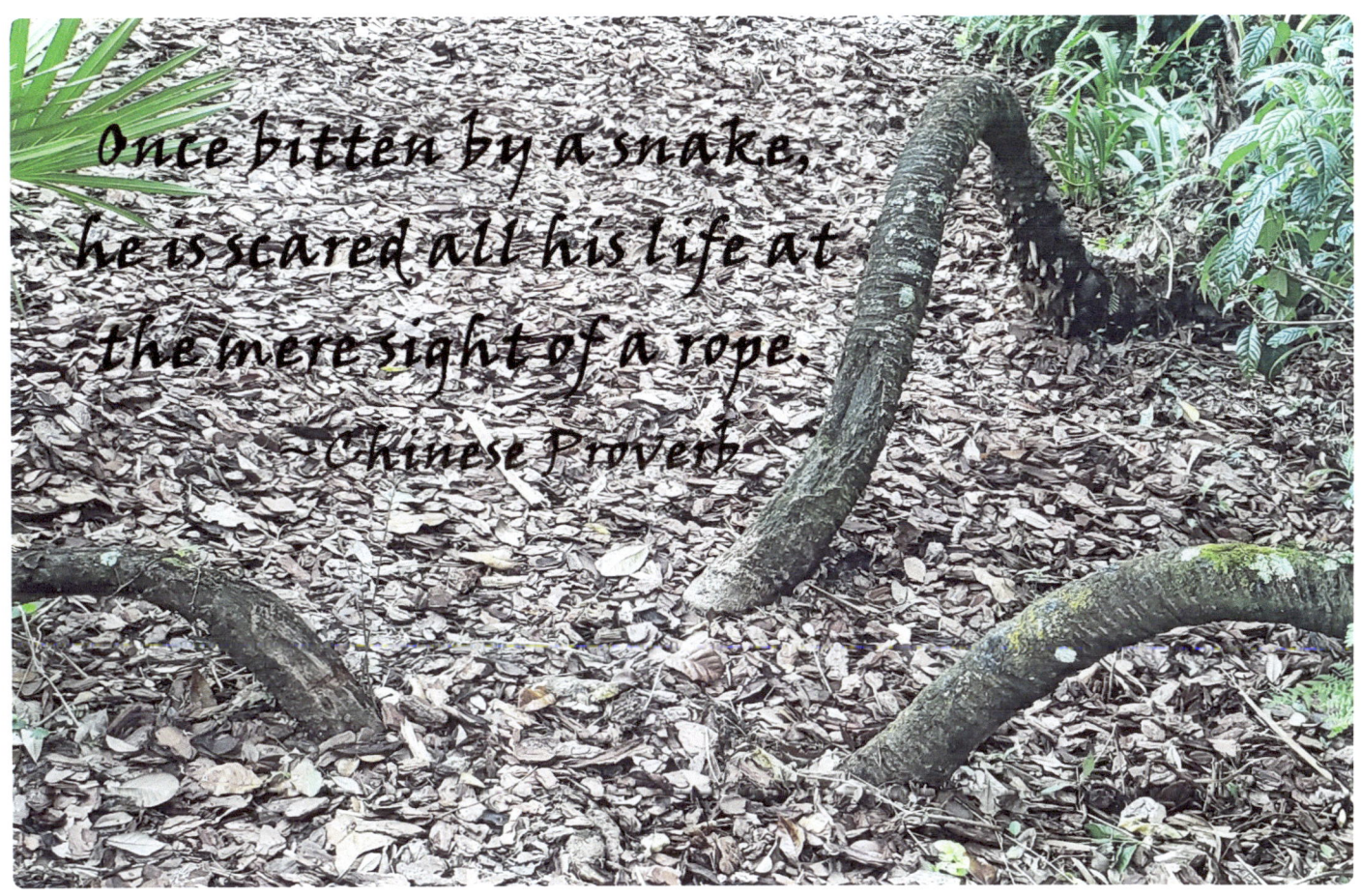

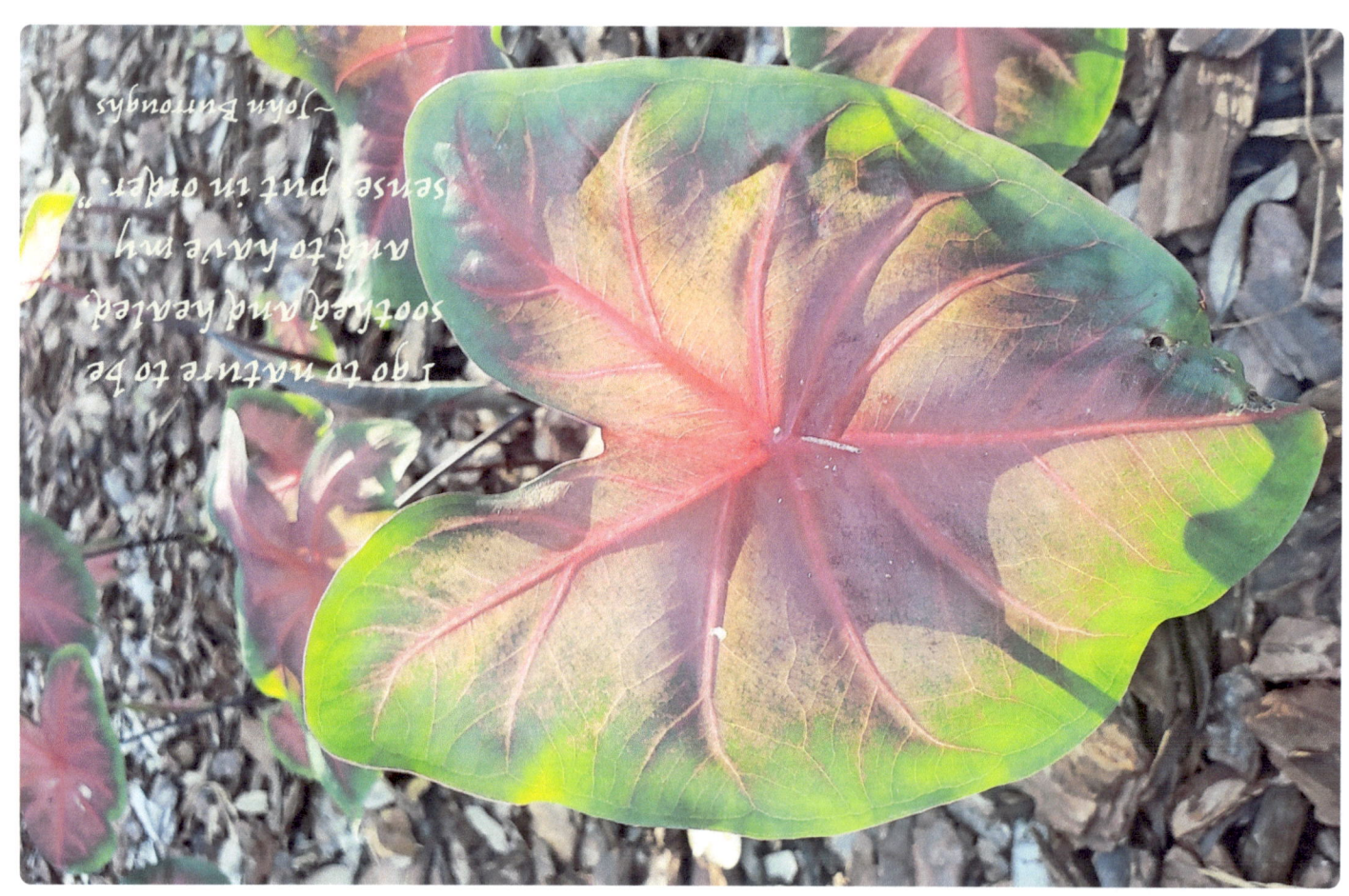

"I go to nature to be soothed and healed, and to have my senses put in order." ~John Burroughs

Pure water is the world's first and foremost medicine.

~Slovakian proverb

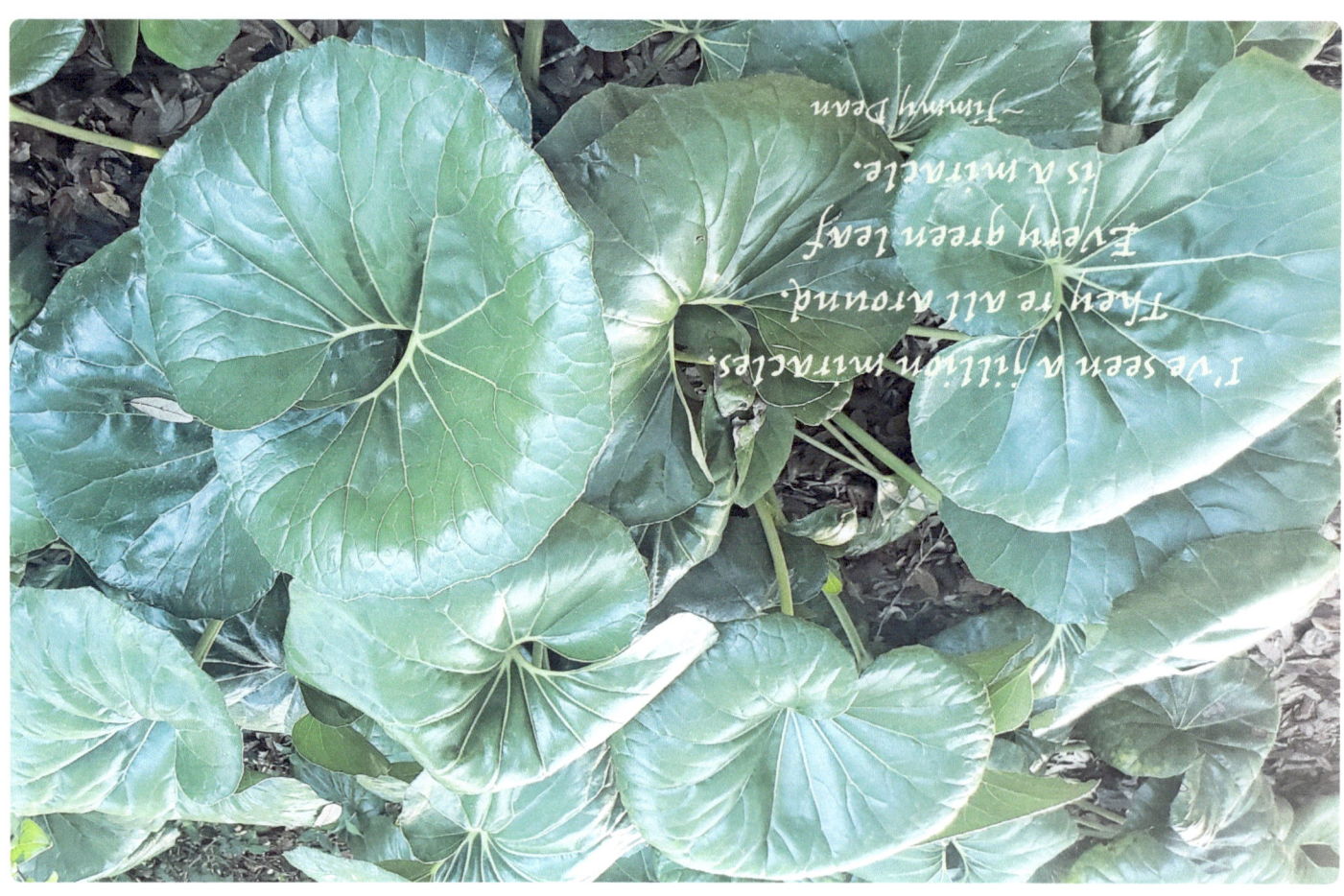

I've seen a jillion miracles. They're all around. Every green leaf is a miracle. —Jimmy Dean

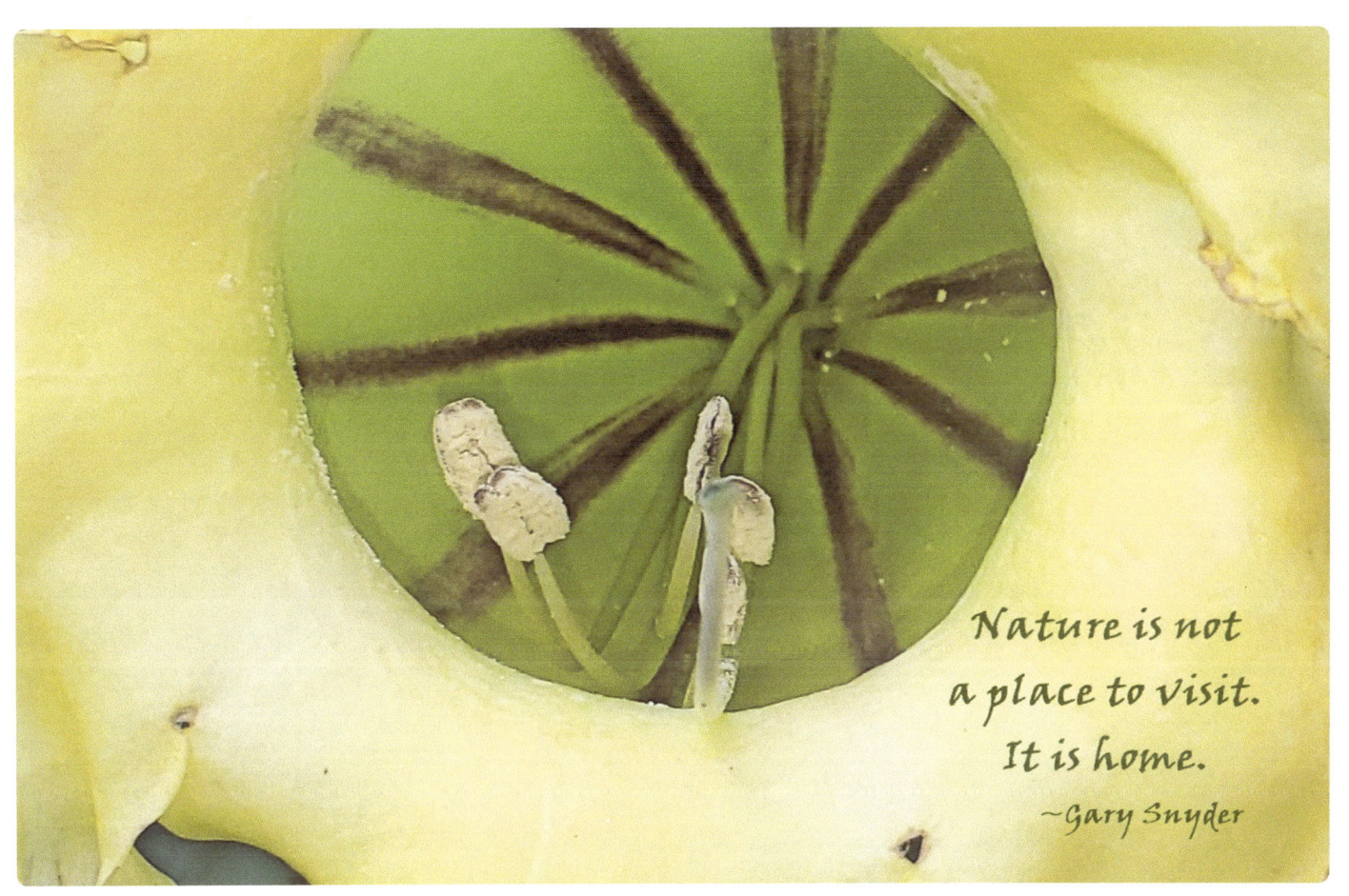

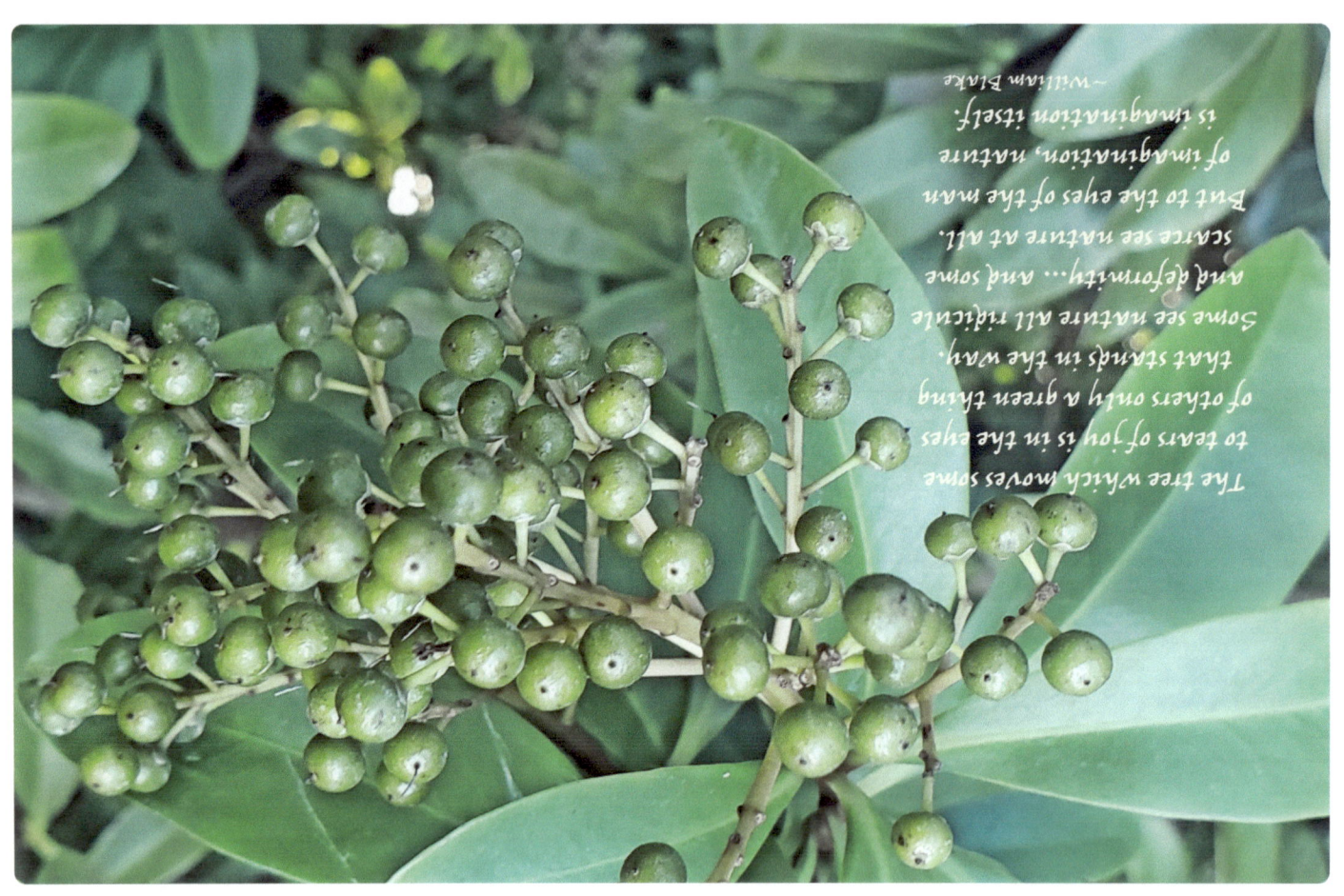

The tree which moves some to tears of joy is in the eyes of others only a green thing that stands in the way. Some see nature all ridicule and deformity... And some scarce see nature at all. But to the eyes of the man of imagination, nature is imagination itself.
~William Blake

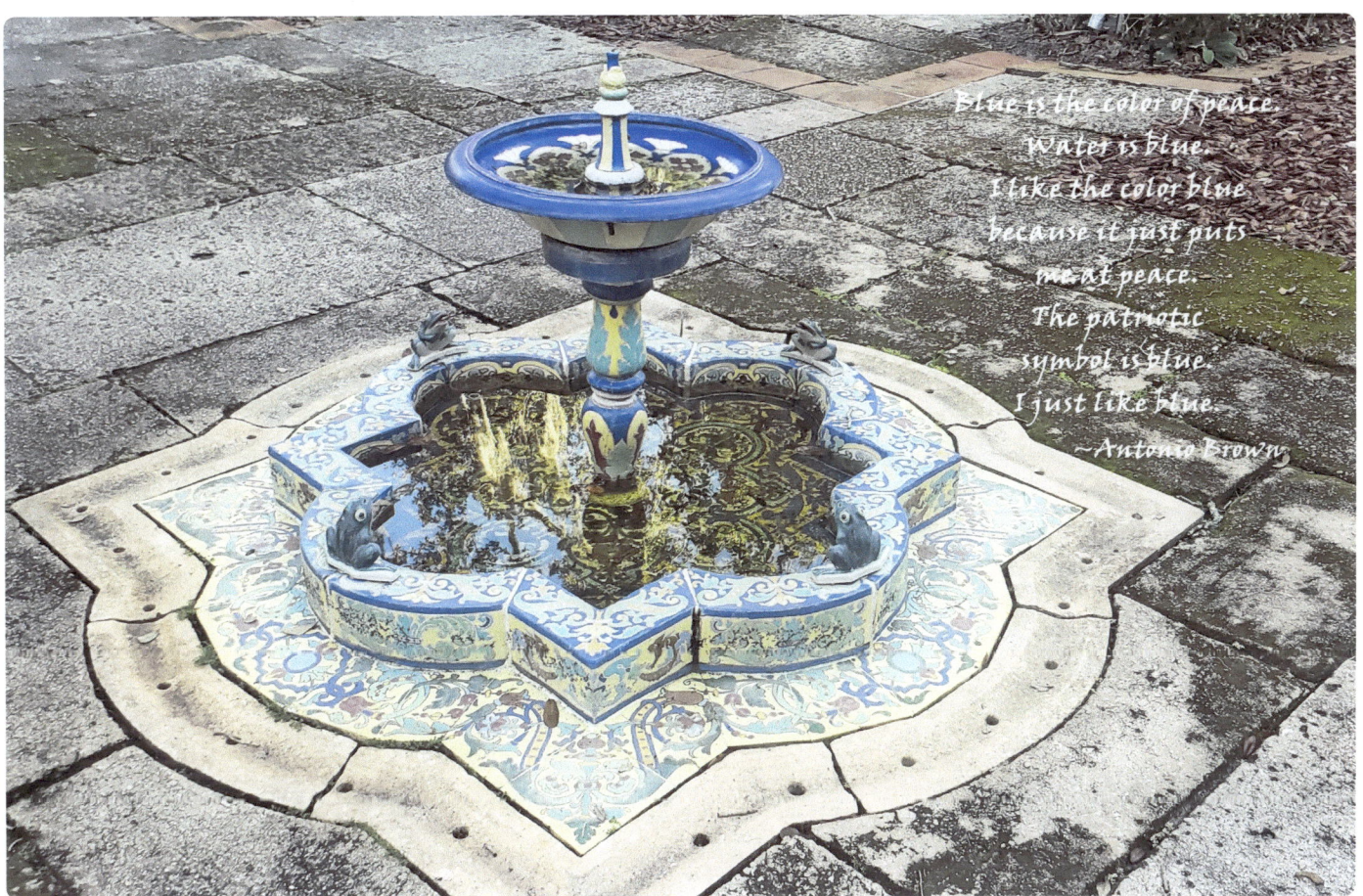

Blue is the color of peace.
Water is blue.
I like the color blue
because it just puts
me at peace.
The patriotic
symbol is blue.
I just like blue.
~Antonio Brown

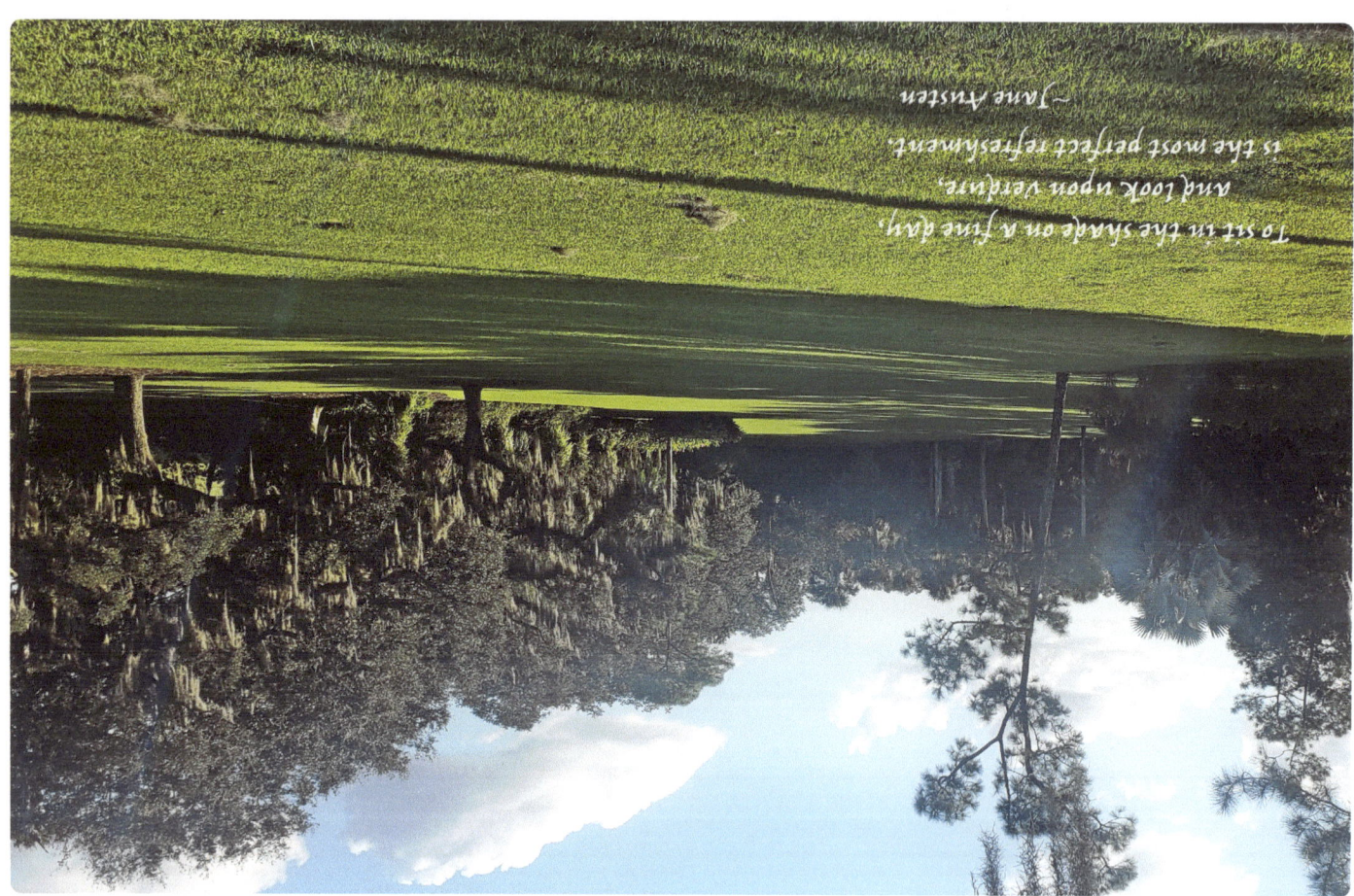

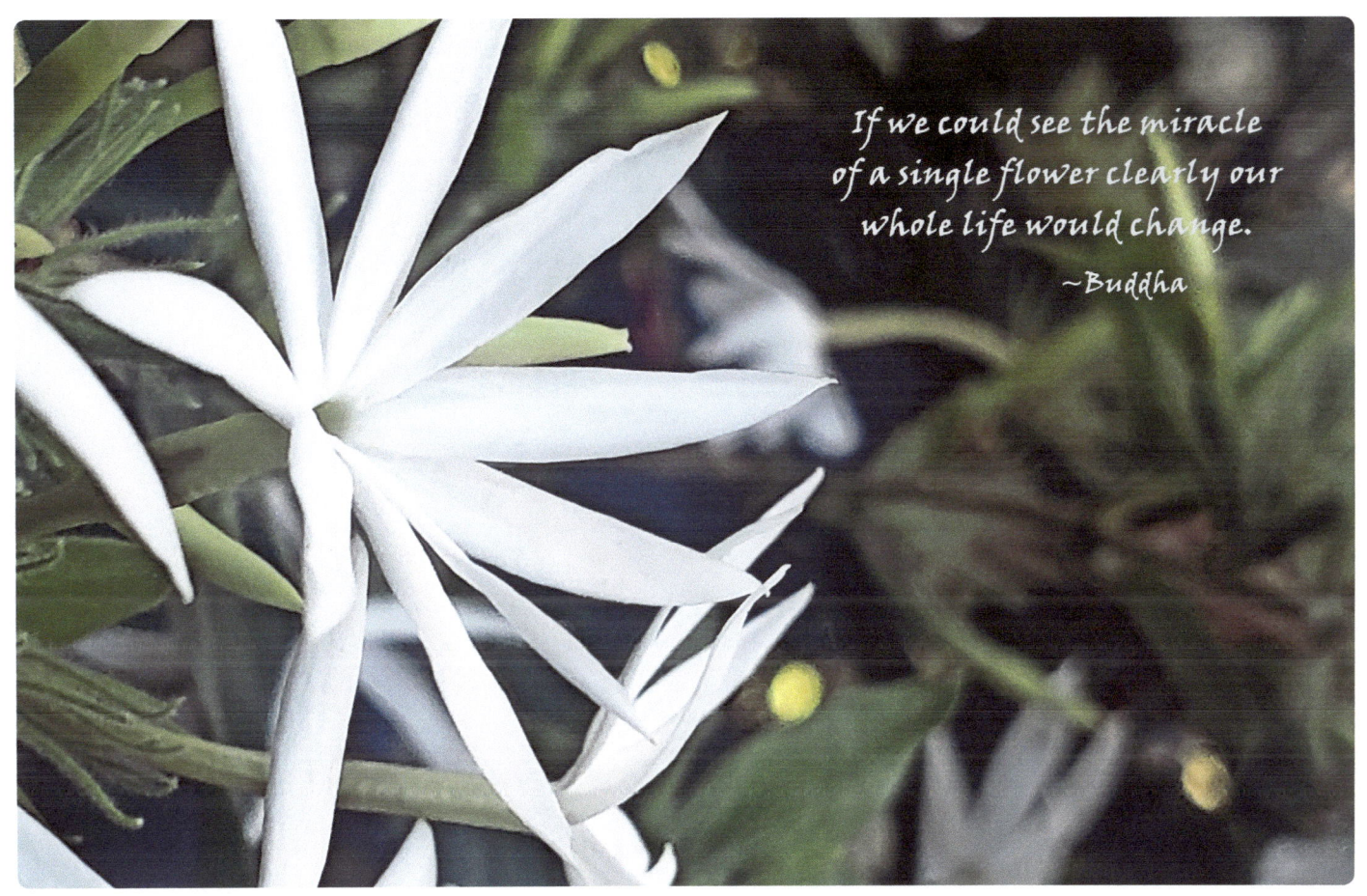

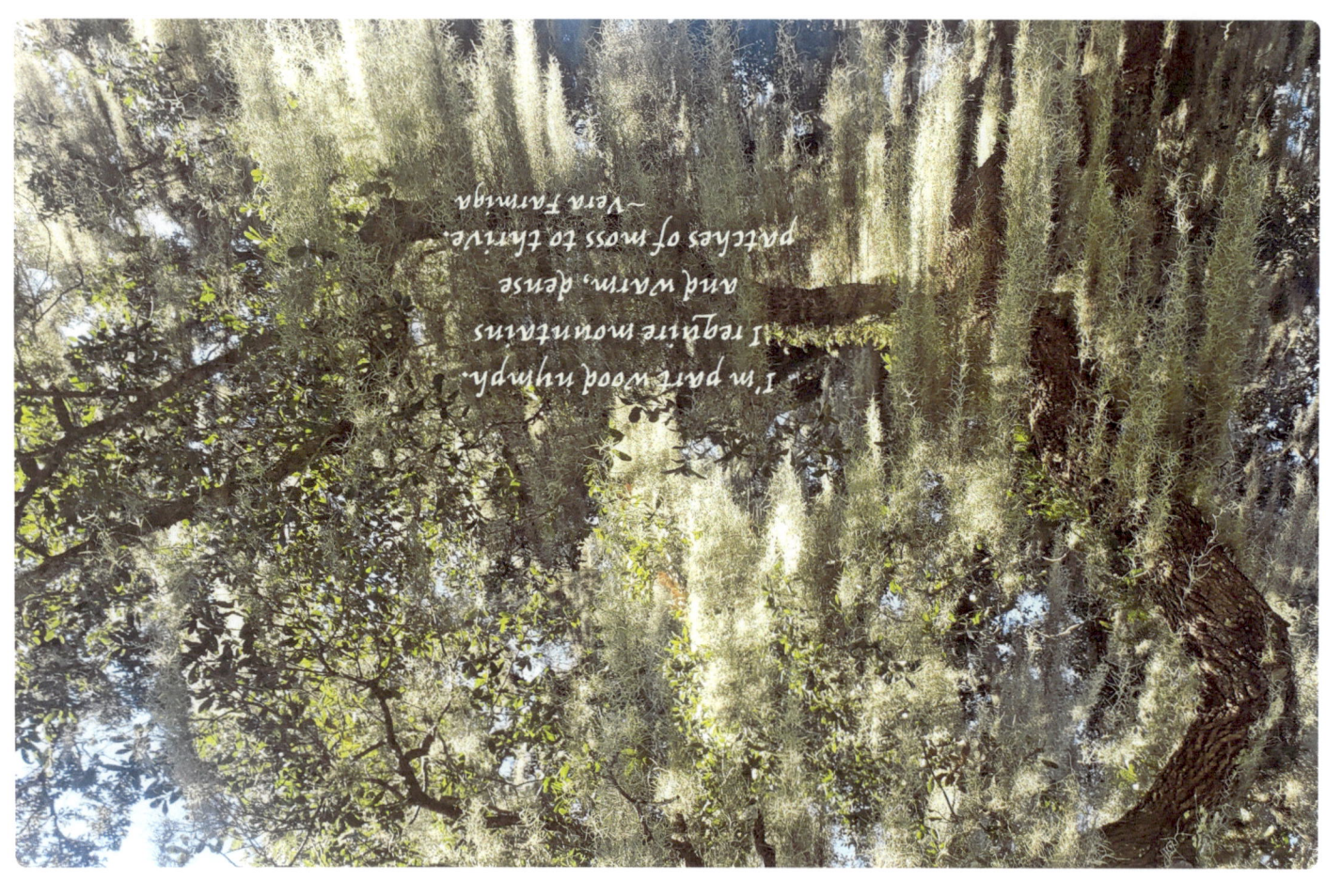

I'm part wood nymph. I require mountains and warm, dense patches of moss to thrive. —Vera Farmiga

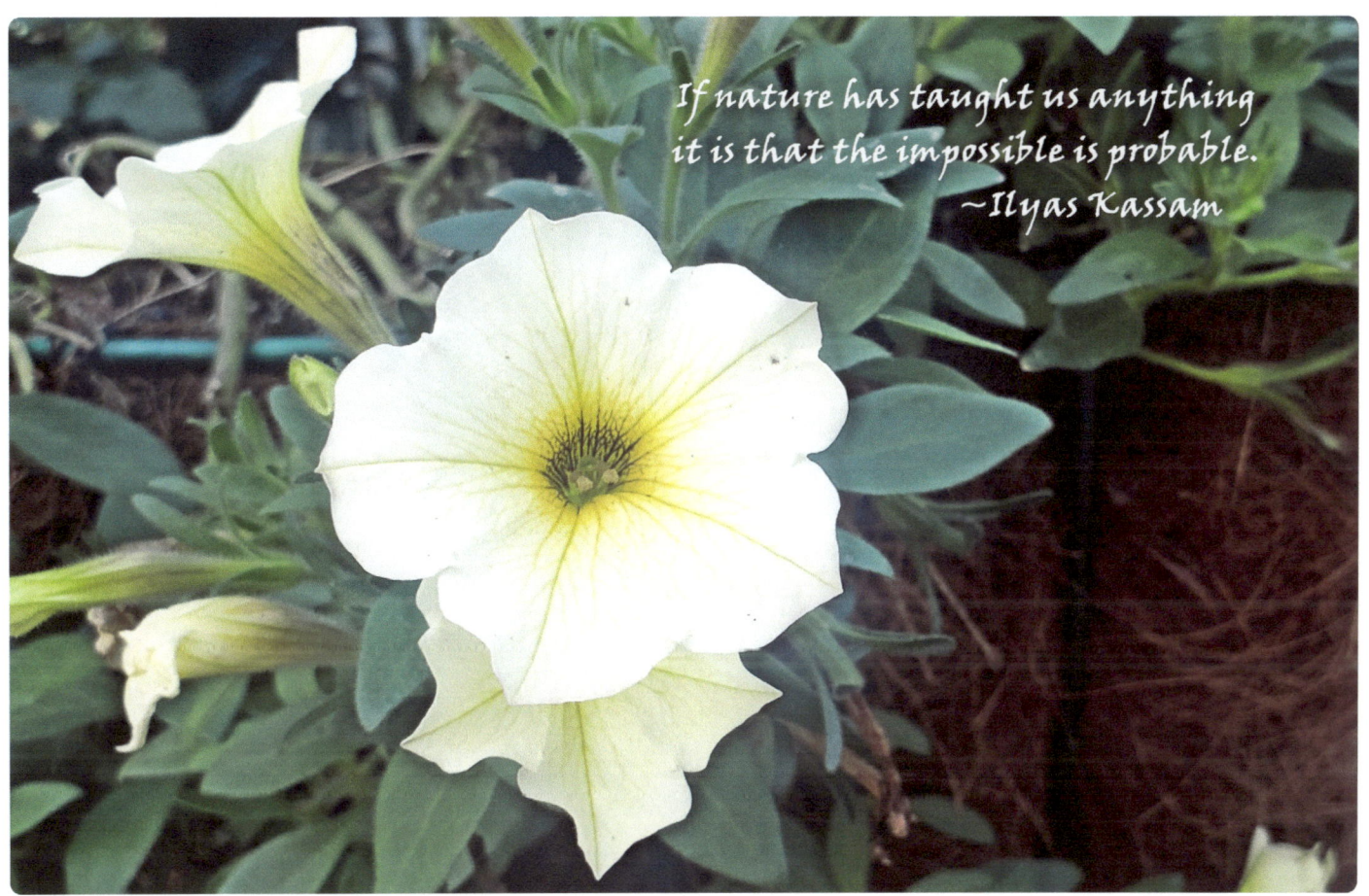

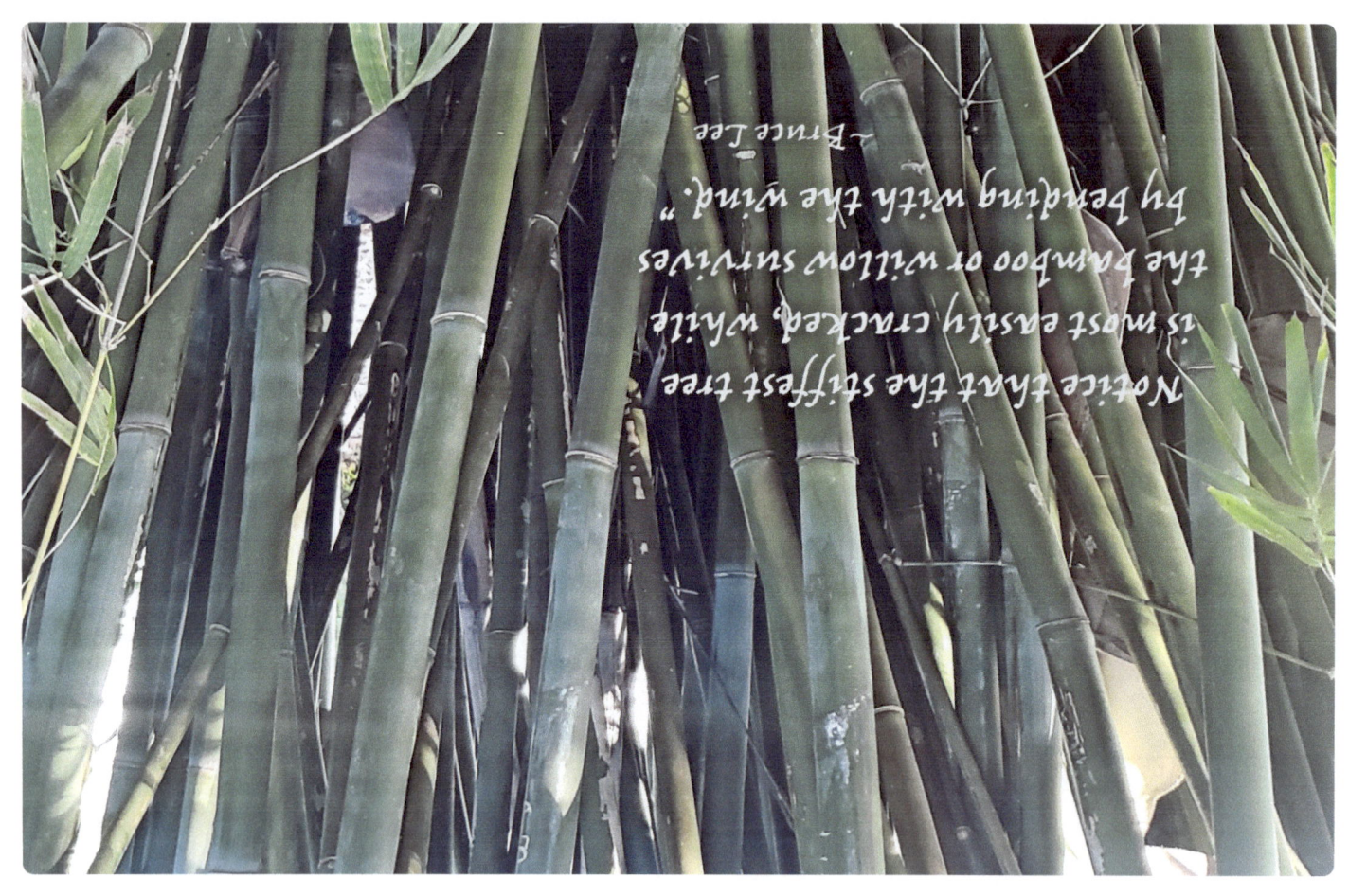

Notice that the stiffest tree is most easily cracked, while the bamboo or willow survives by bending with the wind.
~Bruce Lee

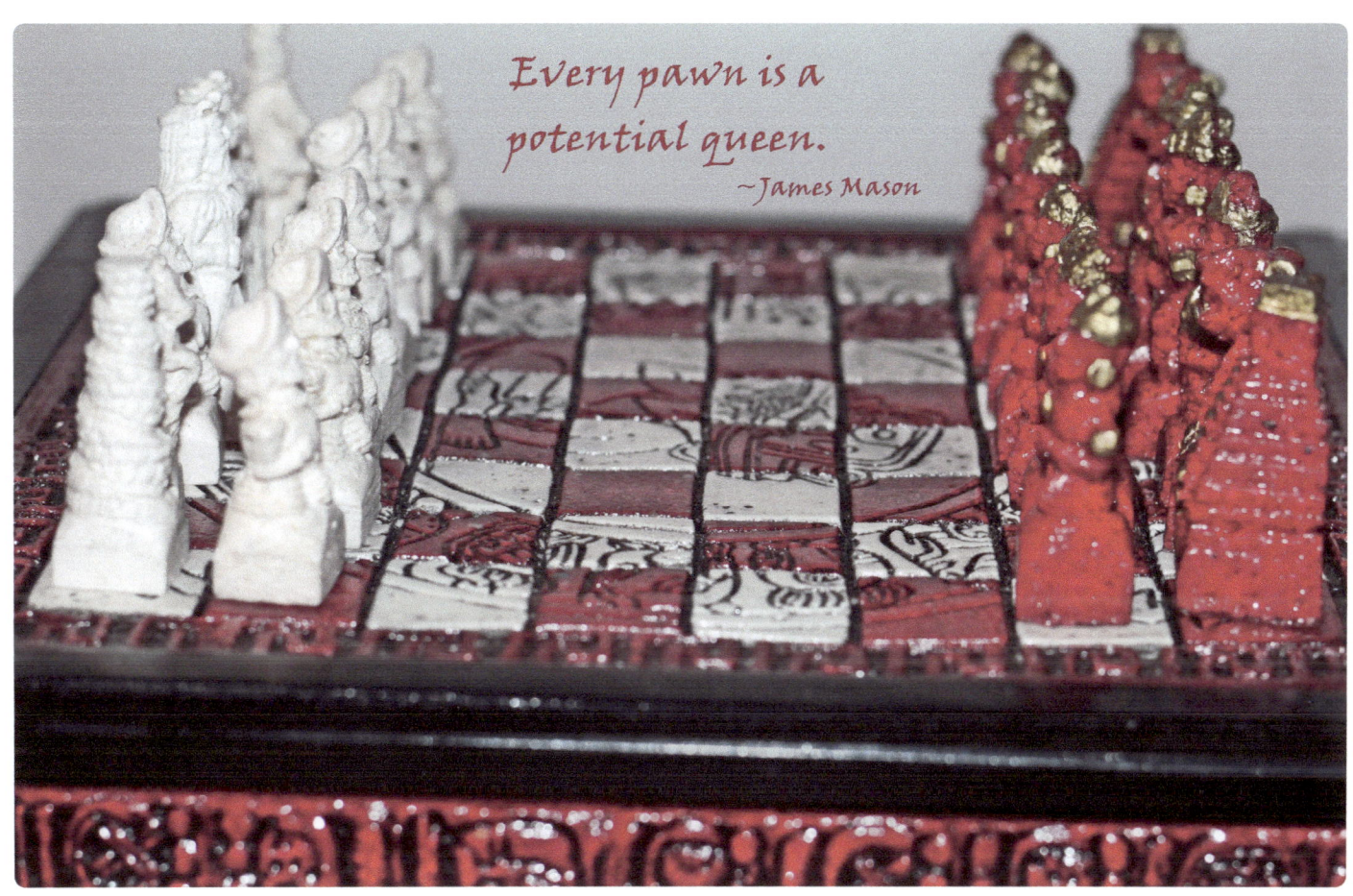

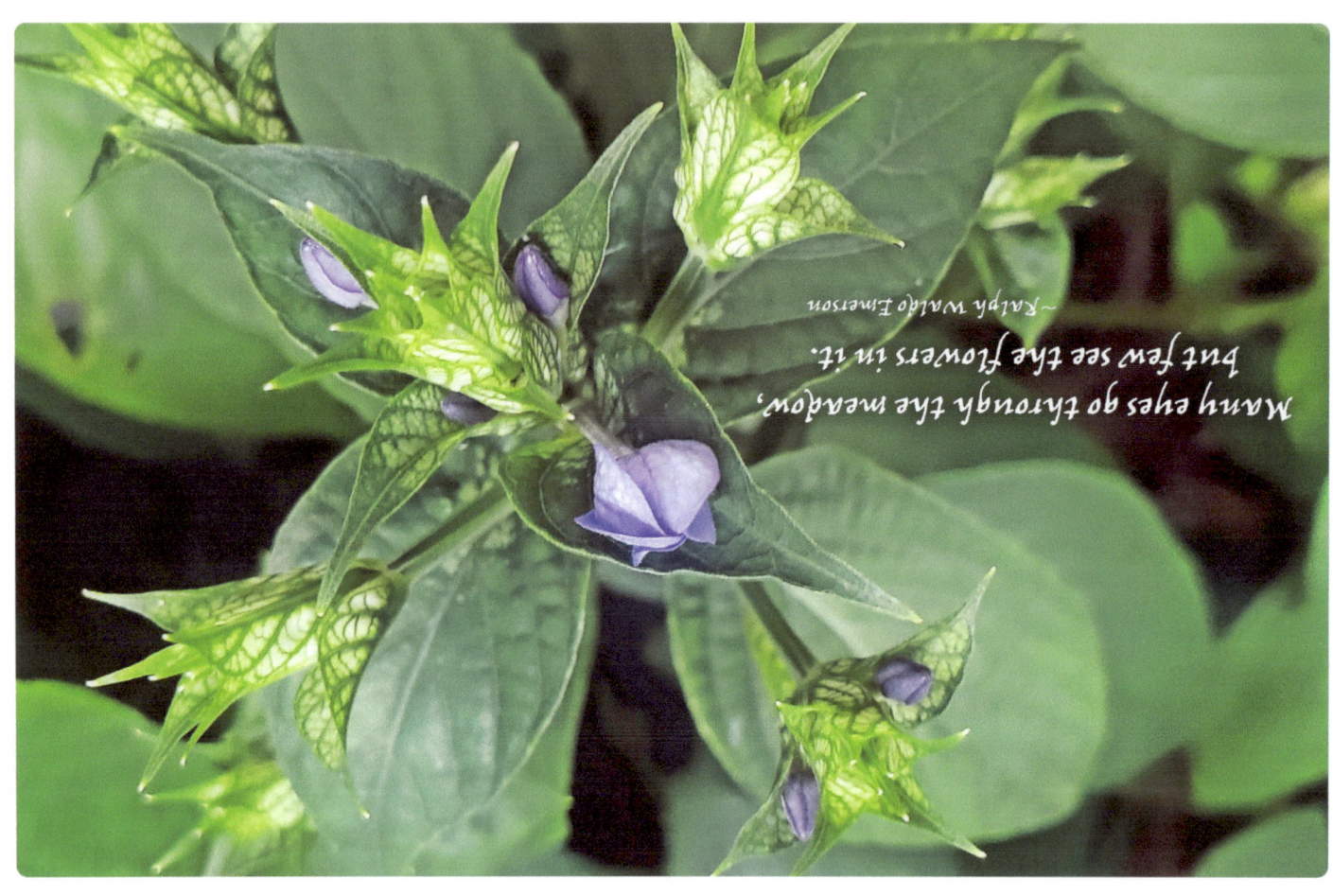

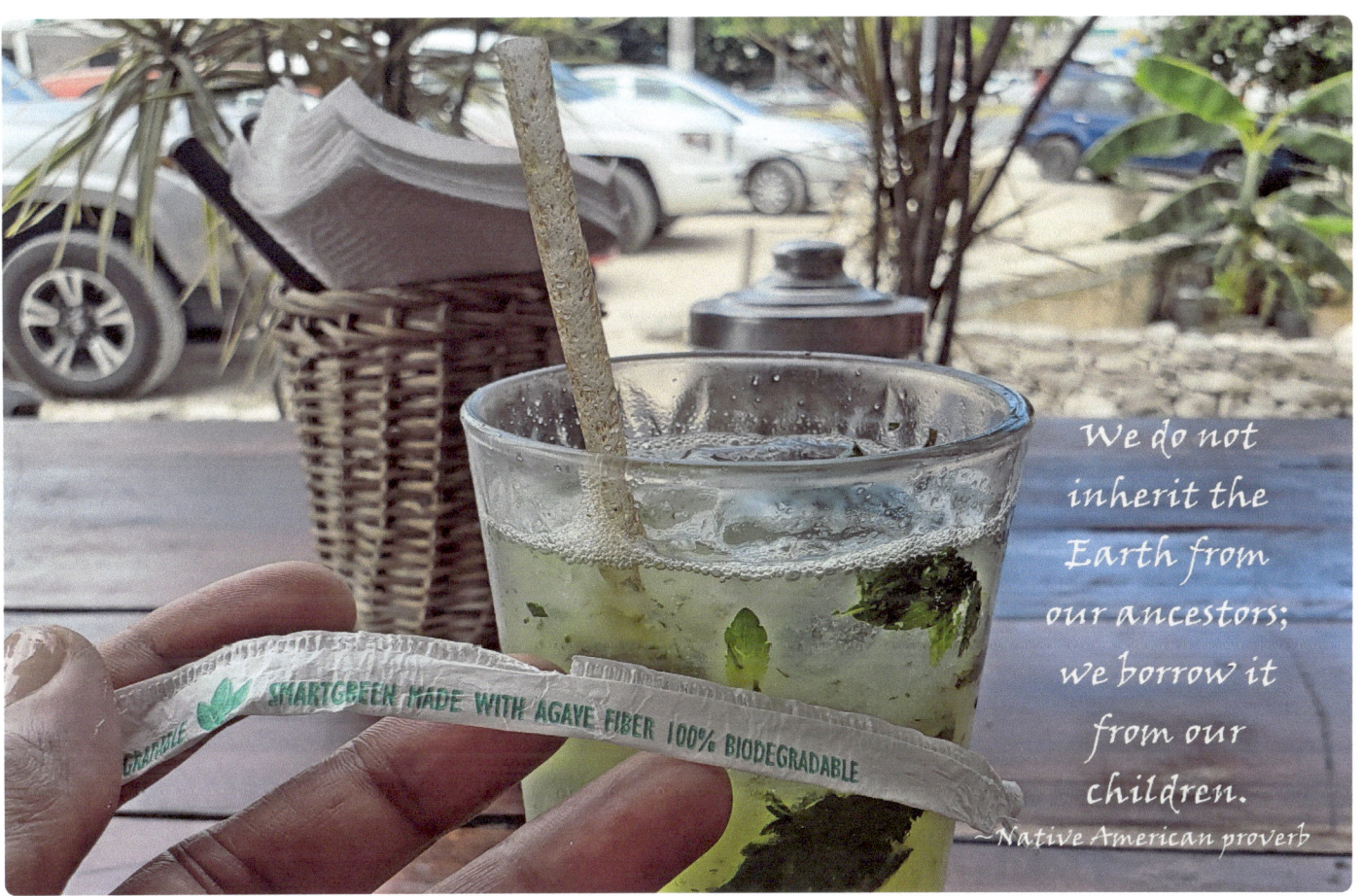

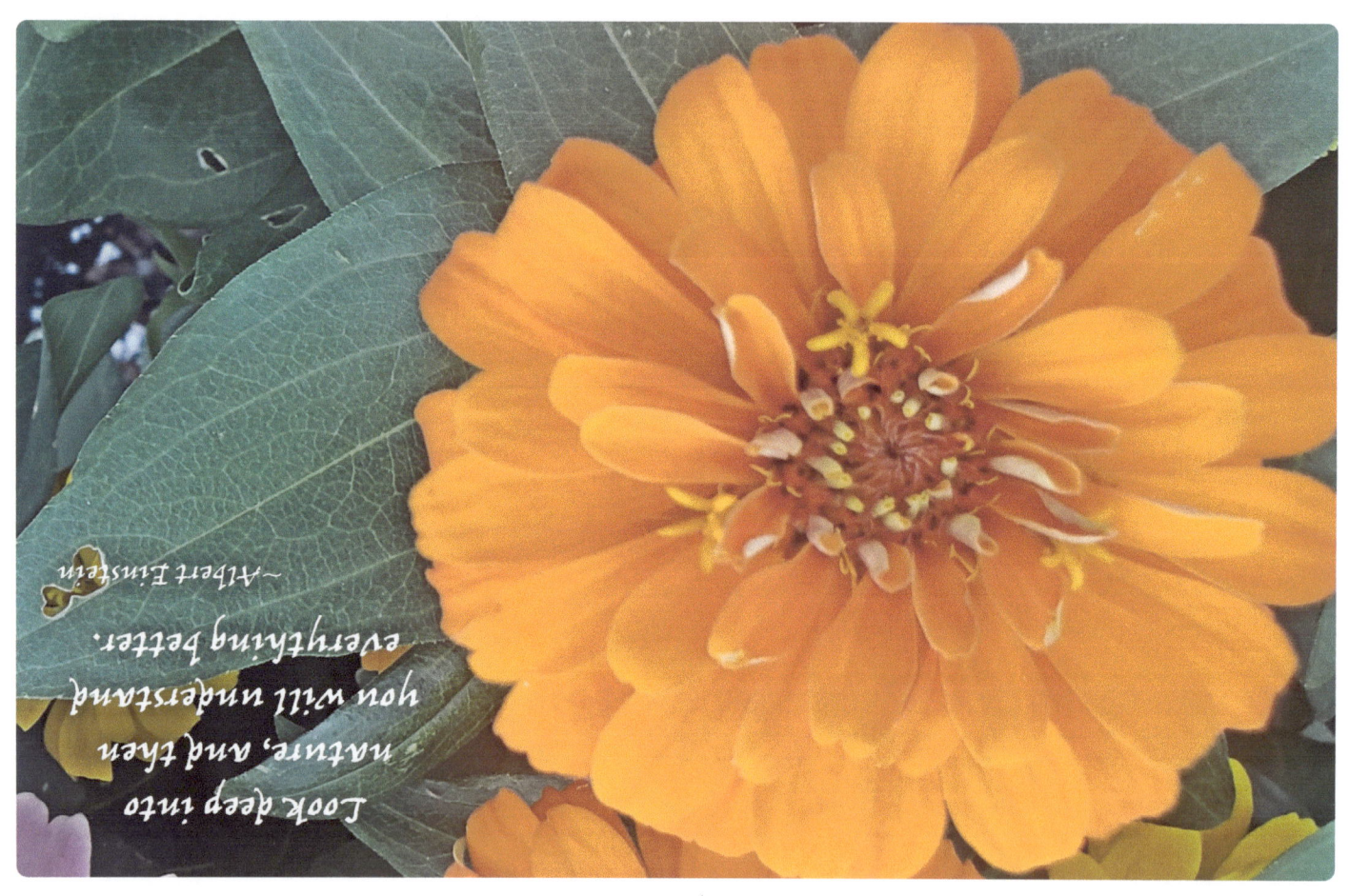

A NOTE FROM THE AUTHOR/PHOTOGRAPHER

Thank you so much for purchasing the first ever Quotos book! Your support is allowing me to pursue my dream of being a professional photographer and published author.

I was born and raised in South Carolina, spent 22 years in Chicago and now reside in Florida where I work as a freelance photographer and author.

In my free time I enjoy traveling, yoga, biking, Scrabble, chess and spending time with my children, family and friends.

If you enjoyed this book, please leave a review, then tag and follow @tolenmedia to be informed when the next Quotos book is released and also for details on buying poster prints of any photos contained herein.

Your contribution for this work will allow me to devote precious time and resources to the next installment of inspiring quotes and more of my own photography. The world can always use more inspiration and smiles.

Thanks again for your support!

Love,
Christopher Conrad Tolen